ECKANKAR
Dictionary

Paul Twitchell

ILLUMINATED WAY PUBLISHING, INC.
P.O. BOX 27088
GOLDEN VALLEY, MN 55427-0088
1-800-457-9063

ECKANKAR Dictionary

Copyright © 1973, 1989 ECKANKAR

Printed in U.S.A.
ISBN: 0-88155-085-X
Library of Congress Catalog Card Number: 90-81506

Second Edition – 1989

First 📖 Printing – 1990

The *ECKANKAR Dictionary* was researched and compiled from the works of ECKANKAR. Pronunciations and meanings are given as used in ECKANKAR and are not to be confused with pronunciations and meanings of other paths and languages.

Pronunciation Guide

SOUND	AS IN	RESPELLING SYMBOL	ECK EXAMPLE
Vowels			
short a	cat	a	Askleposis *ask-leh-POH-sis*
ah sound	father	ah	Banjani *bahn-JAHN-ee*
long a (very close in sound to short e)	made	ay	Harji *HAYR-jee*
short e	pet	eh	Agam Des *AH-gahm DEHS*
long e	tea	ee	Lai Tsi *LIE TSEE*
long i	hide	ie	Lai Tsi *LIE TSEE*
short i	hit	i	Askleposis *ask-leh-POH-sis*
long o	coat	oh	Anami Lok *ah-NAH-mee LOHK*
short o	pot	o	cosmic *KOZ-mik*
ow sound	cow	ow	Outer Master *OW-tehr MAS-tehr* Yaubl Sacabi *YEEOW-buhl sah-KAH-bee*
short u	mug	uh	animus *AH-nee-muhs*
long u	rule	oo	Fubbi Quantz *FOO-bee KWONTS*
Consonants			
b	boy	b	Banjani *bahn-JAHN-ee*
ch	China	ch	Ju Chiao *JOO chee-AH-oh*
d	dog	d	Gopal Das *GOH-pahl DAHS*
f	fat	f	Faqiti *fah-KEE-tee*
hard g	go	g	Gopal Das *GOH-pahl DAHS*
h	hat	h	Honardi *hoh-NAHR-dee*

SOUND	AS IN	RESPELLING SYMBOL	ECK EXAMPLE
j	jam	j	Banjani *bahn-JAHN-ee*
k	keep	k	Katsupari *kaht-soo-PAH-ree*
l	lily	l	Lai Tsi *LIE TSEE*
m	man	m	Towart Managi *TOH-wahrt mah-NAH-gee*
n	no	n	Namayatan *nah-mah-YAH-tahn*
ng	sing	ng	Sohang *SOH-hahng*
p	pat	p	Peddar Zaskq *PEH-dahr ZASK*
qu	quick	kw	Fubbi Quantz *FOO-bee KWONTS*
r	right	r	Rebazar Tarzs *REE-bah-zahr TAHRZ*
s	say	s	Sakapori *sah-kah-POH-ree*
sh	ship	sh	Shariyat *SHAH-ree-aht*
t	top	t	Tindor Saki *TIN-dohr SAH-kee*
th	thin	th	gatha *GAH-thah*
v	voice	v	ECK-Vidya *ehk-VEE-dyah*
w	way	w	Wu Tenna *WOO TEHN-nah*
x	exit	ks	exoteric *ehks-oh-TEHR-ik*
y	yes	y	Yavata *yah-VAH-tah*
z	zipper	z	Shamus-i-Tabriz *SHAH-muhs-ee-tah-BREEZ*

Contents

A

aberrations. A departure from what is right, true, correct, etc.; in ECKANKAR considered as brought about by actions arising out of the FIVE PASSIONS OF THE MIND: LUST, GREED, ANGER, ATTACHMENT, and VANITY.

abheda. *ahb-HAY-dah* Any philosophy which denies the distinctiveness of spiritual and material principles.

absolute immutable law. The laws of the universes which are found in the SHARIYAT-KI-SUGMAD, the holy scriptures of ECK. These laws spell out the vast COSMIC ORDER which manifests throughout every part of the worlds of the SUGMAD. These are the great laws of life, which exist in and by themselves without relation to any other laws and are never changing or varying.

absolute Spirit. SPIRIT not yet differentiated into any specific manner or form; the universal Spirit which indwells in and pervades all things and is at the heart of all appearance; that which is unchanging.

Absolute, the. The SUGMAD; the Supreme God.

absolute truth. The ULTIMATE REALITY; the unchanging isness of the universal SPIRIT, the SUGMAD.

Accessible Realm. The HUKIKAT LOK; highest state SOUL generally reaches; the first realm available to beings, Souls, and entities for dwelling.

achkan. *AHCH-kahn* A knee-length coat with closed collar.

Acolyte. *AH-koh-liet* The first degree of INITIATION in ECKANKAR received by the chela in the DREAM STATE; the CHELA is then put under SPIRITUAL DISCIPLINE at the first stage of responsibilities, prior to acceptance into the reality of the SPIRITUAL WORLDS through the LIVING ECK MASTER.

Adamic Race. *ah-DAH-mik* Another name for the first root race. *See also* POLARIANS.

Adepiseka. *ah-deh-pee-SEH-kah* An INITIATE of the Tenth Circle.

Adept(s). *a-DEHPT* The ECK MASTERS; those who have spiritual proficiency in the art of SOUL TRAVEL and have become a member of the Ancient Order of the Vairagi. *See also* VAIRAGI ADEPTS.

adhar chakra. *ah-DAHR CHAH-krah* The lowest of six nerve ganglions in the spine corresponding with the psychic centers of the lower universe; the seat of the earth element and the first stage of the yogis called the four-petaled lotus. *See also* MUL-CHAKRA.

adharma. *ah-DAHR-mah* An unrighteous act or person; wickedness.

Adhyatma. *ah-DYAHT-mah* Another name for the supreme SPIRIT, the ECK.

adi. *AH-dee* The beginning; the unknown Deity; primal.

Adi-ECK. *AH-dee-EHK* The primal God force; the true force of that spiritual ESSENCE of God by which all life exists.

adi-karma. *AH-dee-KAR-mah* Karma not earned by the individual SOUL; that which was established by the LORDS OF KARMA in the beginning of Soul's journey in the lower worlds. Also called primal karma: action of the CREATIVE FORCE.

Adi-Mahanta. *AH-dee-mah-HAHN-tah* The primordial MAHANTA. The line of mastership begun with RAMA, the first world savior, which has been handed down through the centuries by the ECK MASTERS via oral secret teachings to those who were initiated into the Order of the Vairagi.

aditi. *ah-DEE-tee* The boundless; space; ether; that which has no beginning nor ending; ETERNITY.

Adom. *AH-dohm* The first Polarian man, the Rabi; his female companion was called EDE.

Adonai. *ah-DOH-nie* One of the Hebrew names assigned to the god who was the first tribal deity of the Jews. *See also* YAHVEH.

Adoration Ray. The eighth of the ten forces, or rays, of the ECK which are sent out to the worlds below by the SUGMAD through the ECK.

advaita. *ah-DVAH-ee-tah* The nondual; the nonduality which lies beyond the worlds of duality; that which in ECK is called the true SPIRITUAL WORLDS, the universes of the God Realm; that which is beyond the PSYCHIC WORLDS.

Agam. *AH-gahm* The Inaccessible region; the AGAM LOK, the ninth plane; next to the highest spiritual world known.

Agam Des. *AH-gahm DEHS* Also Agam Desh. A spiritual city on the earth planet located in the HINDU KUSH mountains, whose spiritual leader is YAUBL SACABI. Those who live here are called the ESHWAR-KHANEWALE or God-eaters, and it is visited in the ATMA SARUP (SOUL BODY) by invitation only; inaccessible space.

Agam Lok. *AH-gahm LOHK* The INACCESSIBLE PLANE; the Lord of this world is AGAM PURUSHA; the sound is the music of the woodwinds; the word is HUK. Inaccessible realms are those where there exists no matter, energy, space, or time.

Agam Purusha. *AH-gahm poo-ROO-shah* When the SUGMAD limits ITSELF to some extent, however slightly, IT becomes the AGAM PURUSHA; the ruler over the AGAM LOK, the INACCESSIBLE PLANE.

agate, month of the. In the ECK-VIDYA, this refers to the month of September, the ninth journey of SOUL on the path of TOTAL AWARENESS, or GOD-REALIZATION; DZYANI, the days of friendship. *See also* JOURNEY OF SOUL.

agati. *ah-GAH-tee* The wrong path, as distinct from the right path, or the ECK state of CONSCIOUSNESS, the highest. It is also the word used for rebirth.

Agent of God. A true ECK traveler, the representative of the Spiritual LIGHT, the COSMIC LIGHT, the truth within Itself.

agni. *AHG-nee* Fire and related subjects; one of the TATTWAS, the five PRIMARY STATES OF MATTER, the others being PRITHVI, JAL, VAYU, and AKASH.

Agnotti. *ahg-NAHT-tee* The ECK MASTER in charge of the SHARIYAT-KI-SUGMAD in the Temple of Akash on the AGAM LOK; his title is the MAHAYA GURU.

Ahankar. *ah-HAHN-kahr* One of the four divisions of MIND; the faculty of separating self and self-interest from all else; the I-NESS, the faculty which executes orders. Exaggerated, it becomes VANITY, or AHANKARA. *See also* ANTISHKARANS.

ahankara. *ah-HAHN-kah-rah* VANITY, one of the FIVE PASSIONS OF THE MIND.

ahanta. *ah-HAHN-tah* Selfness or I-NESS; the state of being an EGO.

ahimsa. *ah-HEEM-sah* The doctrine of COMPASSION, oneness, and sacredness of all life, both human and animal.

Ahmad Qavani. *AH-mahd kah-VAH-nee* The LIVING ECK MASTER who was present at the signing of the Magna Charta, during the time of King John of England.

Ahrat. *AH-raht* A superior SOUL; one who has reached the Third INITIATION in ECKANKAR and is known as the worthy one, the KURNAI.

Ahura Mazda. *ah-HOOR-ah MAHZ-dah* A name used in ancient Persia for the state of GODHOOD; ZOROASTER's name for God.

Ajna. *AHJ-nah* The THIRD EYE, or TISRA TIL; the SPIRITUAL EYE or door through which the SPIRITUAL TRAVELERS may pass between the lower and higher worlds on the journey into the God realms.

Akaha. *ah-KAH-hah* The nameless world; the unspoken; the OCEAN OF LOVE AND MERCY; the world of the SUGMAD. *See also* LAMAKAN.

Akal. *ah-KAHL* Designates the supreme SPIRIT, the ECK, as the opposite of the KAL, the negative power; timeless.

Akasa. See AKASHA.

akash. *ah-KAHSH* The highest of the five TATTWAS, the primary sources out of which all material things are created. Also called the ether. *See also* PRIMARY STATES OF MATTER.

Akasha. *ah-KAHSH-ah* The primal matter force; It enters into the composition of all beings and things of life; the primary Sound of every world within the universes of the SUGMAD; the ECK.

Akashar. *AH-kah-shahr* The lord who has real power, the actual king of all; used as the opposite of the DHARAM RAY, the negative power; implies law and order.

Akashar Purusha. *AH-kah-shahr poo-ROO-shah* SPIRIT; the CREATIVE POWER known as the ECK.

Akash Bani. *ah-KAHSH BAH-nee* HEAVENLY MUSIC; Word of God; Sound of the ECK.

Akashic records. *ah-KAH-sheek* The records, memories, and KARMIC PATTERNS of SOUL stored on the Third, or CAUSAL, PLANE for the Physical and ASTRAL WORLDS.

Akeviz. *ah-KAY-veez* A spiritual city in the highlands of Guatemala; one of the smaller communities of SPIRITUAL TRAVELERS who are still connected with the ancient civilization of the Mayans; promotes the ancient mysteries of the once powerful Mayans and AZTEC Indians.

Akivasha. *See* TIRMER; VOICE OF AKIVASHA.

Akshar. *AHK-shahr* The Supreme Deity, the SUGMAD; imperishable.

Alakh Lok. *ah-LAHK LOHK* The INVISIBLE, or Sixth, PLANE; second world of the SUGMAD; the Lord is the ALAKH PURUSHA; the sound here is the wind, sometimes roaring and sometimes gentle; the word is SHANTI.

Alakh Purusha. *ah-LAHK poo-ROO-shah* Ruler of the INVISIBLE PLANE or ALAKH LOK, the sixth plane, the second world of the SUGMAD; the fathomless, incomprehensible, impersonal, invisible; cannot be approached even in thought.

Alam-i-Hutal Hut. *ah-LAHM-ee-HOO-tahl HOOT* The top of the MENTAL PLANE, the ETHERIC PLANE.

Alaya Lok. *ah-LAH-yah LOHK* The ENDLESS PLANE, which lies beyond the ALAKH LOK; the Seventh Plane. The ruler is the ALAYA PURUSHA; the word is HUM; the sound is deep humming.

Alaya Purusha. *ah-LAH-yah poo-ROO-shah* The ruler on the ALAYA LOK, the Endless world, or the seventh plane.

Alayi. *ah-LAY-yee* The word for the PHYSICAL PLANE.

Allah. *AH-lah* Called the merciful God of Islam; the MAHANTA Consciousness as the vehicle for the SUGMAD as It was known to the Muhammadans.

Aluk. *ah-LOOK* The word for the HUKIKAT LOK, the eighth plane.

Aluk, Temple of the. *See* JARTZ CHONG.

Ambica. *ahm-BEE-kah* Goddess of destruction.

Amdo. *AHM-doh* The dialect of a community of persons on the border of Tibet and China; also the name of a large Chinese province and tribe, where ECK has been prominent and well-known.

Ameretat. *ah-meh-reh-TAHT* One of six rays of light from the Divine; immortal life, freedom from DEATH or dissolution. *See also* AMESHA SPENTAS.

Amesha Spentas. *ah-MEH-shah SPEHN-tahz* Holy immortals; the six ways, or rays of light, from the Divine, that the supreme

SUGMAD has to make ITSELF known to man. *See also* AMERE-
TAT; ARMAITI; ASHA-VAHISTA; HAURVATAT; KHASHATHRA-VAIRYA; VOHU-
MANO.

Amma. *AH-mah*   Another name for God.

Anahad Shabda. *ah-NAH-hahd SHAHB-dah*   The Voice that is
that ESSENCE; the Holy Ghost, the comforter, the DIVINE SPIRIT
that gives life to all; the ECK.

Anahad Yoga. *ah-NAH-hahd YOH-gah*   Another name for the
creative Sound; the great sound wave; the still, small voice; the
VOICE OF SILENCE; the ECK.

anahata chakra. *ah-nah-HAH-tah CHAH-krah*   The twelve-
petaled lotus which is focused on the HEART CENTER and represents the destructive power.

Anakamudi Temple. *ah-nah-kah-MOO-dee*   The TEMPLE OF
GOLDEN WISDOM on the ALAYA LOK.

Anami. *ah-NAH-mee*   Without name, nameless. Another name for
God.

Anami Lok. *ah-NAH-mee LOHK*   That plane where SOULS are
reproduced by the Lord of Lords reacting upon ITSELF; the
world of the Supreme Being, the SUGMAD; the mighty center
of the universes, the very heart and core of all life and existence.
The sound here is of the whirlpool, and the Word is HU; the
Tenth Plane.

Anami Purusha. *ah-NAH-mee poo-ROO-shah*   Lord of the tenth
plane, the ANAMI LOK.

ananda. *ah-NAHN-dah*   Bliss or that state of happiness the yogi
reaches in the high MENTAL PLANE. Also known as Ananda Yoga.

Anda. *AHN-dah*   The lowest plane of the Far Country; the ASTRAL
WORLD. *See also* ANDA LOK; ASTRAL PLANE.

Anda Lok. *AHN-dah LOHK*   The ASTRAL WORLD. The sound is the
roar of the sea and the word is KALA. It is the plane of emotion;

the source of flying saucers, spirits, etc.; the highest plane reached by ASTRAL PROJECTION. *See also* ASTRAL PLANE.

Angel of Death. The messenger who takes those who die on this plane to the Astral region where the DHARAM RAYA, the righteous judge, sits enthroned to judge every individual according to his deserts.

angels. Beings above ordinary man who help to serve man in many ways; also called PRETS, DEVTAS, BHUTS, DEVAS, etc. They have great powers and are quite willing to serve people who live in HARMONY with them.

anger. In ECKANKAR, one of the FIVE PASSIONS OF THE MIND. *See* KRODHA.

Anhad. *AHN-hahd* Ceaseless; always. It refers to the music of ECK.

anima. *AHN-eh-mah* Female image in man which produces moods.

animus. *AHN-eh-muhs* Masculine image in woman which produces opinions.

anitya. *ah-NEET-chah* Impermanent; transitory. Opposite of *nitya,* which means "everlasting." Another word for CONTEMPLATION.

antaskarana. *ahn-TAHS-kah-RAH-nah* The ladder of God along which the DEVAS and the angelic forces are continually descending and ascending.

antishkarans. *ahn-TEESH-kah-rahnz* The four divisions, functions, or modes of action of the MIND: CHITTA, MANAS, BUDDHI, and AHANKAR.

Anuga Region. *ah-NOO-gah* A place within the ATMA LOK where the SOUL records are kept for those who have reached the Sixth INITIATION.

Apollonius of Tyana. *ap-eh-LO-neh-uhs uhv TIE-eh-neh* An ECK MASTER in the first century A.D. who saved himself from DEATH by transporting his PHYSICAL BODY.

Arahata. *ah-rah-HAH-tah* An INITIATE of the Second Circle in ECKANKAR; a teacher of ECK SATSANG classes.

Arahata Marg. *ah-rah-HAH-tah MAHRG* The teaching order in ECKANKAR.

Arhirit. *ahr-HEE-reet* The capital city of the SAGUNA LOK, the ETHERIC PLANE, which is the top of the MENTAL, or Fourth, PLANE.

Armaiti. *ar-mah-EE-tee* One of six rays of light from the Divine; immortal life, freedom from DEATH or dissolution. *See also* AMESHA SPENTAS.

Arrians. *ahr-REE-ahnz* A cruel race which will take over the Earth about the year 3500 A.D., later spreading to Mars and VENUS.

Aryans. *AHR-ee-ahnz* Fifth root race (white race); present ruling race.

asanas. *ah-SAH-nahz* Postures or positions used in MEDITATION; the MIND in the spiritual planes.

Asanga Kaya. *ah-SAHN-gah KAH-yah* The title of the guardian of the SHARIYAT-KI-SUGMAD at the TEMPLE OF GOLDEN WISDOM of JARTZ CHONG on the HUKIKAT LOK. KADMON is the guardian.

asava. *AH-sah-vah* That which is known as mental intoxication, the defilement of MIND; the opposite of arhat, the Buddhist ideal state. The four asavas are: KAMA, sensuality; bhava, LUST of life; ditthi, false view; and avijja, IGNORANCE of things of life.

Asha-Vahista. *ah-SHAH-vah-HEES-tah* One of six rays of light from the Divine; the supreme will, manifested in the world. *See also* AMESHA SPENTAS.

ashram. *AHSH-rahm* The place where the disciples of a spiritual master eat, sleep, and live to be near him and to gather to listen to him as often as possible.

Ashta-dal-Kanwal. *AHSH-tah-dahl-KAHN-wahl* The pure Astral Plane where the disciples of the ECK Master meet him in his Radiant body, or Astral body, for travel in the higher worlds. *See also* NABHI CHAKRA.

ashtavadhaza. *AHSH-tah-vah-DAH-zah* The ability to grasp or attend to different matters at the same time, such as, to Soul Travel and operate the physical body at the same time.

Askleposis. *ask-leh-POH-sis* The Temple of Golden Wisdom on the Astral Plane, where Gopal Das, the great ECK Master, is the guardian of the fourth section of the Shariyat-Ki-Sugmad.

asmita. *ahs-MEE-tah* A word which designates the ego, or egotism.

Asoki. *ah-SOH-kee* An ECK Master still living in the same body he inhabited some sixty thousand years before the advent of the Christian calendar. Living near the city of Retz on Venus, he spreads the message of ECK throughout the planets of the physical world.

aspirant. A disciple of ECK; one who attends the ECK Satsang class, aspiring to become a chela eligible for the Second Initiation.

Astik. *ahs-TEEK* In ECK-Vidya, the month of the emerald, January, the days of wisdom; physical being of man; the physical world; also denotes the disciple who is able to read and understand the Shariyat-Ki-Sugmad in the Atma Sarup (Soul body).

Astral body. The Radiant body; the starry body of the Astral Plane, the second plane of the lower worlds; lighter and finer than the Physical body, it is used as the instrument of expression on the Astral Plane.

Astral City. The capital city of the Astral Plane, which lies below a shining mountain, the powerhouse of lights, and is called the City of Lights. *See also* Sahasra-dal-Kanwal.

astral light. The light which flows from and fills all the Astral world; extremely bright and starry in quality; often mistaken for the true Light of God.

astral museum.   The great museum on the ASTRAL PLANE where the inventions of all lower worlds can be found.

Astral Plane.   The Second Plane of the lower worlds, whose capital is SAHASRA-DAL-KANWAL. Also known as SUKHSHAM DESH, which embraces all of the planets and stars. It extends out into space beyond the reach of any telescope. The highest plane which can be reached by ASTRAL PROJECTION. *See also* ANDA LOK.

astral projection.   A term to denote a limited state of out-of-body travel; a form of physical phenomenon which splits off the sheath of the inner bodies to travel inwardly to the ASTRAL, or Second, PLANE just above the physical; an action which could lead to difficulties in the psychic regions, which are a source of delusion.

astral rays.   Out of the powerhouse at the top of the ASTRAL WORLD flow CURRENTS of light which create and sustain all the worlds in the universes; basically made up of seven colors: black, red, green, blue, orange, yellow, and white; each COLOR and ray has different aspects to assist the physical life on the planets.

Astral world.   The SUKHSHAM DESH or the ANDA world, the lowest of the spiritual worlds which lies just above the Physical world. *See also* ASTRAL PLANE.

astral zone.   *See* ASTRAL PLANE.

astrology.   The study of the WHEEL OF THE EIGHTY-FOUR, the ZODIAC, the mechanical force that is the KAL, or negative, aspect of the universe; uses mechanical standards such as charts, etc. to foretell the future, and can only state the prospects of what could take place; the study of births and DEATHS in the lower worlds.

Asu.   *AH-soo*   The vital SPIRIT, the ECK FORCES of life; another name for the ECK.

Asurati Lok.   *ah-soo-RAH-tee LOHK*   The Desert world. The FAQITI MONASTERY TEMPLE OF GOLDEN WISDOM is situated in the Gobi Desert; BANJANI is the guardian of the introduction to the

SHARIYAT-KI-SUGMAD which ECK CHELAS study here in the DREAM or SOUL TRAVEL STATE.

Atlanteans. *at-LAN-tee-ehnz* The fourth root race, the red race, an olive-skinned people who lived upon the continent of ATLAN-TIS.

Atlantis. *at-LAN-tis* Legendary continent which existed in the Atlantic Ocean west of Gibraltar and sank into the ocean when it was destroyed by earthquakes because of its morals, corruption, and degeneration of sex.

Atma. *AHT-mah* SOUL, that spark of divine life which God has placed within the human or other forms to give them existence.

Atma Lok. *AHT-mah LOHK* Also Atma Pad. The Fifth, or SOUL, PLANE, the dividing plane between the psychic and the true spiritual worlds; the plane of SELF-REALIZATION, or SOUL recognition; the word here is SUGMAD, the sound is the single note of the flute, and the ruler is SAT NAM.

Atman. *AHT-mahn* SOUL, the I Am, or the individualized LIFE-FORCE that shares the qualities of the ECK, or the HOLY SPIRIT. *See* ATMA.

Atmanukhs. *AHT-mah-nookz* Those who follow the dictates of SOUL and live in the higher CONSCIOUSNESS, always facing God, knowing life on the earth plane is temporary and that they will be traveling the paths into the higher worlds.

Atma Sarup. *AHT-mah sah-ROOP* The SOUL BODY, the LIGHT BODY; the ATMA SHARIR which dwells on the Fifth Plane; an extremely sensitive body which, in Its natural state, is a perfect vessel of the Divine Being.

Atma Sharir. *AHT-mah shah-REER* The SOUL BODY, or ATMA SARUP.

Atma Vidya. *AHT-mah VEE-dyah* Knowledge of SOUL or spiritual life.

at-one-ment. The SUGMAD AWARENESS of ITSELF as being the oneness of ITSELF: in ECKANKAR, the state of CONSCIOUSNESS reached by the CHELA with the LIVING ECK MASTER, and through him the ECK POWER, in order to reach the God Worlds.

attachment. The state of being connected by ties of affection, attraction, etc., particularly to the karmic conditions of life that hold one in the physical universes; includes ideas, DREAMS, CONSCIOUSNESS of the lower self which creates attachment to the physical realm, DESIRES, and connections with family and possessions.

attavada. *aht-tah-VAH-dah* A false belief in IMMORTALITY; doubt that SOUL exists.

Attitudes, Law of. The fifth law of the physical universe, or Law of the States of Being; the power of IMAGINATION rules over will in the actions in this universe. *See* LAWS OF THE PHYSICAL UNIVERSE.

Audible Life Stream. Also Audible Life CURRENT. The Divine Being expressing ITSELF in a ray, both audible and visible, like a radio wave flowing out from the supreme creative center of the Universe of Universes; LIFE-FORCE that can be heard and seen with the spiritual vision and objective sight of materialism; the all-embracing spiritual force of the SUGMAD, which composes life and makes up all elemental substances including the component parts of SOUL; the ECK.

Aum. *AHM* or *ah-UHM* Word for the MENTAL PLANE; also the sound; used by yoga and Hindu religious groups; a part of the ECK SOUND CURRENT.

aura. *AHR-ah* The magnetic field surrounding a person which is composed of an EMANATIVE SPHERE of thought forces and emotions collected around the physical frame in the form of fine vibratory waves or rays of COLOR; white is the true spiritual power; yellow is the color of SOUL POWER; indigo, INTUITION; blue, wisdom; green, energy; orange, health; red, life-force.

avabahda. *ah-VAH-bah-dah* Waking perception; DISCRIMINATION.

Avatar. *AH-vah-tahr* The World Master; the savior of the human race. One is always present in the physical realm guiding the human races.

Avernus. *ah-VEHR-nuhs* The dark realm of the Astral Plane, where many Souls who have spent their earth lives in evil deeds must spend time. Referred to as the Seven Worlds of Avernus; Hades; Hell.

avidya. *ah-VEE-dyah* Ignorance of truth; a lack of enlightenment; unenlightened.

avyakta. *ah-VYAHK-tah* Unmanifested; the uncaused cause of material, phenomenal existence.

Awagawan. *ah-wah-gah-WAHN* Incarnating of Soul; rebirth. Age-long cycles of life and death, transmigration and reincarnation; the wheel of life. *See* Wheel of Awagawan; Wheel of the Eighty-Four.

awakened Soul. Soul functioning in the spiritual worlds while still living in the physical state in Its physical body.

awareness. In ECK, the movement of the inner being to know; realization in the consciousness, brought about by being certain of receiving; realization or recognition of the power within.

Awaz. *ah-WAHZ* Another name for ECK, the Sound Current.

ayatana. *ah-YAH-tah-nah* The twelve sources of mental processes.

Ayur Vedha. *AH-yoor VAY-dah* The ECK system for renewing the body's health to look and feel younger. *See* Kaya Kalp.

Aztecs. *AZ-tehkz* Descendants of the race which once inhabited the sunken continent of Atlantis. *See also* Akeviz.

B

Babla Mohenjo. *BAH-blah moh-HEHN-joh* Living ECK Master during the reign of Constantine. He had a small school for ECK chelas near Constantinople, and was at the Council of Nicaea called by Constantine in Bithynia, Asia Minor, during 325 A.D.

baibek. *BIE-behk* The practice of discrimination, the first step that one reaches on the path of ECKANKAR. *See also* viveka.

baikhari. *BIE-khah-ree* The oral teachings.

Baju. *BAH-joo* Chant or word for the Etheric Plane.

Balance, Law of. The stability which lies in the Godhead: all is completely in balance in God's universal body. The principle of unity, of oneness, but in the lower worlds this unity is simulated by the interchange between pairs of opposites. *See* Polarity, Law of.

Bani. *BAH-nee* The heavenly music; the ECK, which is the Audible Life Stream; the melody which is given by the SUGMAD through the ECK; the Light and the Sound.

Banjani. *bahn-JAHN-ee* ECK Adept and guardian of the Shariyat-Ki-Sugmad in the Faqiti Monastery Temple of Golden Wisdom on the Asurati Lok (Desert world) in the Gobi Desert.

Baraka Bashad. *bah-RAH-kah bah-SHAHD* May the blessings be.

bardo. *BAHR-doh* In Tibetan Buddhism, the place between the Physical and Astral worlds through which Soul must pass after It leaves the physical body; the purgatory of the Christians.

B

being. That which is, as distinguished from that which is not. The assumption or choosing of a category or identity.

beingness. SOUL is the manifested individual beingness of the ECK SPIRIT, which has been created out of this Spirit, with the ability to have FREE WILL, to make Its own choices, to be able to have opinions, INTELLIGENCE, IMAGINATION, and to postulate and create. *See also* ATMA.

Be-ness. The pure Being; means God, the true One, the transcendental aspect of the ULTIMATE REALITY; the SUGMAD.

bhajan. *BAH-jahn* The spiritul exercise of listening to the music of the ECK; that ability to listen to the HEAVENLY MUSIC within with the spiritual ears.

Bhakta. *BAHK-tah* A disciple; one who is devoted to his Master. The Fourth INITIATON; *See* CHIAD.

Bhakti. *BAHK-tee* Love which is inseparable from life itself; devotion to the Master; an INITIATE of the Seventh Circle. *See also* SHAB.

Bhakti Marg. *BAHK-tee MAHRG* The ECK order of love.

Bhakti Yoga. *BAHK-tee YOH-gah* The yoga of devotion; discards all rites and ceremonies and seeks union with the ECK through the force of love only.

Bhanwar Gupha. *BAHN-wahr GOO-pah* The ETHERIC PLANE; home of the LORD SOHANG, through whom the great power CURRENT flows into this region and downward.

Bhavachakra. *BAH-vah-CHAH-krah* The cycle of the ECK-VIDYA or the wheel of life. There are twelve major experiences of SOUL on this wheel of life, or Bhavachakra. *See* JOURNEY OF SOUL.

bhavana. *BAH-vah-nah* Self-development by any means, but especially by the methods of the MIND; control, concentration, and MEDITATION, the lower aspects of self-development.

B

Bhava Sagar. *BAH-vah sah-GAHR* The tumultuous ocean of birth, DEATH, and rebirth.

bhoa. *BOH-ah* Feeling; particularly for a person or the Master.

bhuts. *BOOTS* Beings in the subtle region close to the earth; a kind of ANGEL above ordinary man who helps to serve man in many ways. *See* ANGELS.

Bihangham Marg. *bee-HAHNG-hahm MAHRG* An accelerated method of reaching the God Worlds; movement of INSTANT PROJECTION into any state of CONSCIOUSNESS; one of the SPIRITUAL EXERCISES OF ECK.

Bihanwi. *bee-HAHN-wee* A great crisis in the unfoldment of spiritual CONSCIOUSNESS.

Bij Sharir. *BEEJ shah-REER* The seed body; the CAUSAL BODY in the Third, or CAUSAL, PLANE; also known as the KARAN SHARIR.

bilocation. The ability to be in two places at the same time; in ECKANKAR accomplished by the use of the SOUL BODY, not as astral travel.

bireh. *BEE-reh* Separation; an internal longing for God.

bloodstone, month of the. *See* JOURNEY OF SOUL; UTURAT.

Blue Light. *See* MAHANTA.

Blue Star. *See* MAHANTA.

bodhi. *BOH-dee* ENLIGHTENMENT; a spiritual condition of a CHELA; a high state which is a few degrees lower than that of the MAHANTA.

Bodhisattva. *boh-dee-SAHT-vah* One who is on the way to attaining perfect knowledge and still has a number of births to undergo before becoming the perfect Master.

Book of Laws. Fundamental laws that govern this universe through SPIRIT once taught to the people by the ECK sage,

B

Mksha, 35,000 years ago in the Indus Valley. *See* Laws of the Physical Universe.

Book of Life.   An enormous book miles in length, width, and thickness; entries are made by mammoth Angels when a Soul reincarnates. It is the Book of Records that the Lords of Karma examine to determine the just merits due a person at the time of Death.

borders of heaven.   Coming into the Awareness of the threshold of the Invisible, the unseen, the unknown, which is called heaven.

Boucharan.   *BOO-chah-rahn*   Order of ECK Adepts.

Bourchakoun.   *boor-chah-KOON*   Those known as the Eagle-eyed Adepts; the Living ECK Master; the Adepts of the Ancient Order of the Vairagi. *See also* Vairagi Adepts.

Brahm.   *BRAHM*   The ruler of the three worlds of Vedanta, Buddhism, and Hinduism. Spoken of as the Great Brahman in the Hindu sacred writings; Kal Niranjan, or the negative power. *See* Trinity of the Hindus.

Brahma.   *BRAH-mah*   Creative member of the fourth region; accepted by most Hindus as the Supreme Deity; one of the three currents flowing out of the Brahm Lok world; creation. *See also* Trinity of the Hindus.

Brahmanda.   *brah-MAHN-dah*   One of the grand divisions of creation, which extends from Trikuti above the Astral Plane to Bhanwar Gupha.

Brahmanda Lok.   *brah-MAHN-dah LOHK*   The Causal Plane, ruled by Brahm; all the karma and records of Souls which reincarnated from life to life are here; the sound is of the tinkling of bells; the plane of negative reality which affects all below.

brahmandi.   *brah-MAHN-dee*   One of the two worlds of the Mind; the other is the pindi; both are used to carry on the business of the world with the help of Soul.

B

Brahm Lok. *BRAHM LOHK* The MENTAL, or Fourth, PLANE, home of the Universal MIND Power; ruled by BRAHM, the negative power.

Bronze Age. *See* DWAPARA YUGA.

Brothers of the Leaf. *See* FIFTH INITIATION; MAHDIS.

Buddhi. *BOO-dee* One of the four parts of the MIND; the INTELLECT proper; chief instrument of thought, DISCRIMINATION, decision, and judgment. *See* ANTISHKARANS.

Buddhi Sharir. *BOO-dee shah-REER* The body which lies between the MENTAL BODY and SOUL; part of the MIND body which acts as a sheath between mind and Soul; very sensitive to impresssions from Soul so as to receive and transmit them between mind and Soul and vice versa.

Buddhism. *BOO-dizm* The path of eight steps concerned with the mental regions; founded by Siddartha Gautama, who became the Buddha Consciousness.

Buika Magna. *BOOI-kah MAG-nah* The remote mountain range in northern Tibet where the KATSUPARI MONASTERY is located.

Bytag, The. *BIE-tahg* A collection of poems by FUBBI QUANTZ, the ECK MASTER at the KATSUPARI MONASTERY in Tibet.

C

C

caitanya. *KIE-tahn-yah* A Hindu expression for CONSCIOUSNESS or INTELLIGENCE; the universal intelligence, or SPIRIT.

Castrog. *KAH-strahg* The LIVING ECK MASTER on ATLANTIS who came there to warn the people of the dangers of practicing black MAGIC and how this would lead to DEATH and destruction under the waters of the sea. He was slain for his troubles.

Causal Body. The memory body, or BIJ SHARIR; corresponds to the CAUSAL PLANE where memories and karmic patterns are stored.

Causal Plane. The Third Plane on the path of ECKANKAR where memories and KARMIC PATTERNS are stored; corresponds to the CAUSAL BODY, or BIJ SHARIR. *See also* BRAHMANDA LOK.

causation. The wheel of life, which is a factor in the human and spiritual cycles of lives; KARMA.

Cause and Effect, Law of. The Law of Karma which works deeply within the individual; one of the most important of the twelve great laws by which the universes are sustained; preserves all the consistencies of life and action. *See* KARMA, LAW OF.

Cave of Fire. Part of the experiences which each SOUL must go through in the lower worlds in order to gain spiritual maturity to return to and become a worker in the spiritual realms.

celestial Light. That LIGHT which surrounds any mystical or ESO-TERIC vision that one might witness.

C

cetana. *seh-TAH-nah* A term for will, known for karma-producing impulses or volitions. *See also* SANSKARAS.

chaitanya. *CHIE-tahn-yah* The embodiment of all attributes of life, of spiritual ENLIGHTENMENT, of vitality and vibrancy; INTELLIGENCE as opposed to materialism; the awakened CONSCIOUSNESS.

chakra(s). *CHAH-krah* A wheel. Refers to the psychic centers in the ASTRAL BODY, which look like a wheel; is divided into parts which are similar to the petals of a lotus flower; correspond with the nerve centers in spine, neck, and head of man; the MICROCOSMIC CENTERS in the body of man which correspond to some portion of the outlying universe or MACROCOSM. *See also* ADHAR CHAKRA; ANAHATA CHAKRA; CROWN CHAKRA; DODAL CHAKRA; HRIDA CHAKRA; INDRI CHAKRA; KANTH CHAKRA; MANIPURAK CHAKRA; MULCHAKRA; NABHI CHAKRA; SAHASRA-DAL-KANWAL; SHIVA-NETRA; SWADHISTANA CHAKRA; VISHUDHA CHAKRA.

channel, divine. In ECKANKAR, used as expressing the state of CONSCIOUSNESS whereby the individual has aligned himself in life and love, which is the ECK, so that he then becomes a distributor for and as the ECK.

chant. *See* MANTRA.

char-dal-kanwal. *CHAR-dahl-KAHN-wahl* The microcosmic center within the body which supplies the fourfold ANTISHKARANS, the mental faculties of the MIND, with centers of action; with four petals, it is the lowest of the six centers in ANDA, and lies nearest to PINDA, the lowest grand division. *See also* MICROCOSMIC CENTERS.

charity. One of the three main qualities of SPIRIT, the other two being freedom and WISDOM; nonattached love.

Chaurasi. *chah-oo-RAH-see* Wheel of the Eighty-Four; the AWAGAWAN, wheel of life and DEATH. *See* WHEEL OF AWAGAWAN; WHEEL OF THE EIGHTY-FOUR.

chela. *CHEE-lah* A student, disciple, or follower of the ECKANKAR spiritual teacher.

Chiad. *chee-AHD* The INITIATE of the Fourth Circle in ECKANKAR; the INITIATION of the intellectual or MIND realm whose function is thought and the evolution of intelligence; mind, CONSCIOUSNESS, and INTELLIGENCE are the ruling factors on this plane; the highest initiation of the PSYCHIC WORLDS, the BHAKTA.

Chitta. *CHEE-tah* One of the four functions, or modes of action, of the MIND; that function, or faculty, which takes cognizance of form, beauty, COLOR, rhythm, harmony, and perspective, receiving its impressions mostly through the eyes. *See also* ANTISHKARANS.

Chiva. *CHEE-vah* The GURU, teacher, or spiritual superior who meets with the student, or CHELA, in the NURI SARUP, the LIGHT BODY, or ASTRAL BODY.

chosen one, chosen people. Those who, through SELF-DISCIPLINE, have reached the state of CONSCIOUSNESS whereby they are acting as godly instruments through which the ECK flows to the world and uplifts all life.

Christ Consciousness. In the Occidental world, COSMIC CONSCIOUSNESS; entering into the KINGDOM OF HEAVEN.

Chu-Ko Yen. *CHOO-koh YEHN* A Chinese LIVING ECK MASTER during the time of Confucius. He is now a spiritual guide on the ALAKH LOK.

clairaudience. The psychic ability to hear sounds and voices regardless of distance.

clairvoyance. The state of seeing and knowing in the PSYCHIC WORLDS; travel in this state is only on the PHYSICAL PLANE.

Clarion. *KLAYR-ee-ahn* A planet where higher evolved SOULS are living to help carry on the work of God throughout the universe.

Clemains. *kleh-MINZ* A ruthless race which will try to destroy everything of the former civilization in the years around 7000 A.D., and will try to set up a new religion based on the idea of priest-kings.

C

Cliff Hanger. A social protester who hangs on the cliffs of Nirvana, safe from the crowd, more outside than an outsider and happier than angry young men, knowing that there is hope for man.

Code of Ethics. *See* Ethics, Law of; Manu Samhita.

cognition. Knowing coupled with awareness and judgment; the grasping of knowledge by the faculty of awareness which is passed on to the body senses for action.

color. Each of the bodies of man, or his modes of consciousness, are related somewhat to the basic primary colors of red, blue, and yellow, which symbolize the Physical body, the Mental body, and the Soul body. Color comes out in the form of fine, vibratory waves, or rays of light. *See also* aura.

compassion. That love which gives of itself freely to all and is not limited, such as the love of the Living ECK Master for all; to suffer with the sufferer. A supreme virtue of ECKANKAR.

conditions of existence. Circumstances and qualities of life, or apparency, reality, and livingness; being, doing, and having.

conscience. The state of moral or ethical development which comes from spiritual unfoldment; the way the SUGMAD keeps man on the path of right conduct for the good of his fellow man.

conscious mind. That part of the intellectual, logical knowing, or awareness, of the individual as opposed to the unconscious mind, or automatic, unawareness.

consciousness. That state of being in which the individual lives daily, which is divided into two parts, the phenomenal and the transcendental. The phenomenal depends upon the sense organs for its expression; the transcendental is independent of the physical senses and works directly with the ECK. Dhyanic consciousness represents a higher state than either of these; the two are in union with each other and with the ECK consciousness, the universal God Spiritual Essence. Reality of a particular kind of awareness which is independent of the mind's activity.

consciousness, individual. *See* individual consciousness.

Consciousness, Law of. The recognition, or realization, of the BEINGNESS of self or thing in thought, which manifests external life and form.

contemplation. In ECKANKAR, a spiritual exercise during which the attention is focused upon some definite spiritual principle, thought or idea, or upon the LIVING ECK MASTER; differs from MEDITATION in that the definite object or vision gives purpose to the focusing of attention, and is active, rather than passive as in meditation.

Copper Age. *See* DWAPARA YUGA.

cosmic altar of God. The inner CONSCIOUSNESS shaped as needed in each individual case; that AWARENESS or point at which the individual surrenders to the ECK.

cosmic basic principle. SOUL operates only in the present moment; not in the past nor the future, but now. The present is everything.

cosmic Being. The solidarity plus the separate individualities of SPIRIT, the whole of It; the whole universe; Spirit, the SUGMAD; God. *See also* COSMIC FORCE.

cosmic consciousness. Spiritual AWARENESS; the state of constant life; the first phase of awareness toward reaching SELF-REALIZATION; ENLIGHTENMENT of the intellectual senses in the Mental realm; main feature of Hinduism.

cosmic current. *See* COSMIC FORCE; ECK.

cosmic eggs. Eggs from which life-forms came forth, planted by the ECK, as the beginning of life and form in the lower worlds.

cosmic force. The ECK, the COSMIC SPIRIT, the body of glory, the SOUND CURRENT; that which is in all life, giving existence to all things.

cosmic goal. Oneness with the great God of all things, an orbit which cannot be deviated from, and which will eventually take SOUL into the higher heavens.

cosmic history. A MAHAYUGA, or MANVANTARA, which is the cycle of the existence of CREATION. It is made up of four YUGAS, or ages: the SATYA YUGA, the TRETYA YUGA, the DWAPARA YUGA, and the KALI YUGA.

cosmic Light. The LIGHT which brings WISDOM, love, and bliss to those who receive It in Its purer form. It may come as a rosy glow or as a fierce, blinding brilliancy around that being It has chosen as Its CHANNEL. *See* COSMIC VIBRATIONS.

cosmic mind. The SUBCONSCIOUS MIND of man which is under the control of the master POWER and through which pours DIVINE WISDOM stored there for release into the CONSCIOUS MIND at the proper time.

cosmic order. The justly and celestially regulated affairs of worlds, nations, and individuals brought about by the ABSOLUTE IMMUTABLE LAW of Cause and Effect. *See also* KARMA, LAW OF; CAUSE AND EFFECT, LAW OF.

cosmic power. The creative, invisible substance which contains all things. *See also* COSMIC FORCE.

cosmic principle. God is one, and this one is centered in each individual.

cosmic process. The limitless differentiation by the POWER of the creative source from the Infinite, the source of all things; the CREATION of forms, action, and INDIVIDUALITY in the worlds of creation by the creative SPIRIT, the ECK, out of the formless creative substance.

cosmic realization. The AWARENESS of Self and the spiritual heights by SOUL, which can be gained through the practice of SOUL TRAVEL. *See also* SELF-REALIZATION.

cosmic sea of life. Trillions of undeveloped SOULS, composing what seems to be a sea, the love CURRENT which is always moving into the lower worlds of space, time, and motion.

cosmic sleep. The state of unawareness through which those SOULS must pass who have not reached spiritual realization

C

when this CREATION is destroyed at the end of the KALI YUGA. After a period, which will last as long as creation did, these Souls will awaken into another golden era of the worlds of matter, energy, time, and space.

cosmic Sound Current. *See* COSMIC FORCE; COSMIC SPIRIT; ECK.

cosmic Spirit. The first positive factor in the whole of CREATION; the combined qualities of negative and positive; the invisible POWER which concentrates the primordial ether into forms and endows those forms with various modes of motion. *See also* COSMIC FORCE; ECK.

cosmic tree. A symbol denoting the life of the cosmos, its consistency, growth, proliferation, generative and regenerative processes; inexhaustible life; it is equivalent to a symbol of IMMORTALITY; the concept of life without DEATH, absolute reality.

cosmic universe. The worlds of CREATION, action, form, and animated life up through the highest spiritual level. *See also* CREATION.

cosmic vibrations. Waves of LIGHT and Sound made up of spiritual atoms. *See also* COSMIC LIGHT.

cosmic wisdom. An AWARENESS of SOUL that It is part of the greater Self, that which is called the SUGMAD or God, and that It is the god of Its own universe and a god among other gods.

cosmic worlds. *See* COSMIC UNIVERSE.

Council of the Nine. The nine unknown ECK MASTERS; the guardians of ECK and Its distribution in the lower worlds.

Co-worker with God. One who takes his place in the guardianship of the beings and entities throughout the worlds of God; voluntarily gives great love and COMPASSION to the worlds.

creation. The finished worlds, established for the purpose of providing a training ground for SOUL. Its original is within each Soul, and all is within the SUGMAD. The worlds of energy, matter, space, and time created by the sound of HU, the WORD,

C

the ECK SPIRIT, and sustained by It. The product of MIND knowing expressed in form by mind thinking.

creative action. That doingness which comes out of AWARENESS of being the image and likeness of God.

creative activity. Doing something of a spiritual nature, besides existence in the materialistic worlds, in order to develop spiritual sensitivity.

creative Current. The LIGHT AND SOUND, life and POWER which flow from SUGMAD to create, govern, and sustain all worlds.

creative cycle. That which starts, changes, and stops with each rest point. Requires the combination of the negative and positive streams, and their complete stillness to achieve the lack of motion which gives the complete static of pure life.

creative energy. *See* COSMIC FORCE; COSMIC SPIRIT; ECK.

creative force. That which connects man with the supreme Deity; the Sound; the WORD; the ECK, the SPIRIT of HU, the LIGHT and the Sound. *See also* ECK.

creative level. Where new laws begin to manifest themselves in a new order of conditions, transcending past experience.

creativeness. The POWER of the ECK; Sound, or vibration, as in the creative Word; the creative and destructive sounds, which can be used to create or destroy.

creative power. SPIRIT; identical with life, love, beauty, and WISDOM; comes from the divine source; manifested by thought; possible because of the CONSCIOUSNESS of oneness of the individual with Spirit, by both the individual and Spirit.

creative principle. Imagining from the end; accepting that you already have that which is desired; acceptance or centering in some state and viewing the world from that state; visualizing from the state desired.

creative process. *See* COSMIC PROCESS.

C

creative ray. One of the ten rays, or forces, which are sent out to the worlds below; the fifth of the ten rays. *See* ECK RAYS.

Creativity, Law of. Every atom is striving continually to manifest more life; all are intelligent, and all are seeking to carry out the purpose for which they were created.

creativity of beingness. That which is seeking for expression, the perfect livingness of SPIRIT; the purpose to be the more perfect expression of Spirit as that which It is, which is life.

creator. The ECK rules as the creator from the positive end of all the universes; the KAL NIRANJAN, or negative force, rules, or is the creator, from the negative pole of CREATION. Both are the MANIFESTATION of the supreme creator coming into manifestation as the ECK, considered as the first personification of the supreme One.

crown chakra. The SUSHUMNA, the thousand-petaled lotus, at the top of the head; the last place for SOUL to leave the body, and the easiest place to succeed with SOUL TRAVEL. *See also* SAHASRA-DAL-KANWAL.

Current. The lines of energy, negative and positive, which form the ECK, the one supreme and infinite energy. The movement of the ECK in the lower worlds; the AUDIBLE LIFE STREAM, the SOUND CURRENT, the ECK, the WORD of God.

cycle, interdiluvian. *See* INTERDILUVIAN CYCLES.

cycle, life. The incarnating of SOUL from birth to DEATH and into life again.

cycle, major. *See* CYCLES OF TWELVE.

cycle, minor. The DOCTRINE OF REINCARNATION; many small cycles working within one MAJOR CYCLE. *See also* CYCLES OF TWELVE.

cycle of balance. The entering of SOUL into the oneness with Its own other self; the coming together of the male and female principle, the negative and positive, so that Soul is complete within Itself.

cycle of cosmic history. *See* COSMIC HISTORY.

cycle of Lhokhor. *See* LHOKHOR, CYCLE OF.

cycles, doctrine of. *See* DOCTRINE OF CYCLES.

cycles of time. Recognized as measured by the clock and calendar in seconds, minutes, hours, days, months, years, three years, six years, and twelve years.

cycles of twelve. The great cycles; each twelve symbolizes a cycle of evolution and experience; it takes in all the threes which are the inner cycles; the active principle of all life MANIFESTATIONS. The number twelve is expressed in the world in the person of the MAHANTA, the LIVING ECK MASTER as humanity as a whole passes through the GREATER CYCLE. Each great cycle of twelve is a new period of starting over again developed only through the LIGHT of the Mahanta, the Living ECK Master who is the embodiment and expression of the twelve. *See also* LHOKHOR, CYCLE OF; RAB-JUNG, CYCLE OF.

D

Dakaya technique. *dah-KAH-yah* The first of the Master techniques; the second is Suang-tu. Used by the ECK MASTERS of the Order of the Vairagi for SOUL TRAVEL.

dama. *DAH-mah* To subdue the passions and restrain the MIND and its DESIRES.

Damcar. *DAHM-kahr* One of the SPIRITUAL CITIES of ECKANKAR, located in the Gobi Desert. The purpose of the ECK MASTERS who live here is to serve the LIVING ECK MASTER.

danda. *DAHN-dah* SELF-DISCIPLINE; sometimes called the Law of Life. The DIVINE RIGHTS of people as well as kings; works both ways, neither can trespass upon the other's rights; righteous law.

Dap Ren. *DAP REHN* The spiritual name of Darwin Gross, the 972nd LIVING ECK MASTER from 1971 to 1981.

dark night of Soul. The arid period that SOUL goes through during which It believes God has forsaken It. It is one of the stages through which every Soul passes on Its way to SELF-REALIZATION and GOD-REALIZATION.

Darshan. *DAHR-shahn* There are two parts of the Darshan: meeting with the Master outwardly and being recognized by him, and meeting with him inwardly and traveling with him; seeing and being seen by him, and the ENLIGHTENMENT which comes with this act.

dasa-bhumi. *DAH-sah-BOO-mee* A stage of WISDOM through which CHELAS pass.

Daswan Dwar. *DAHS-wahn DWAHR* The TENTH DOOR, the subtle opening in the head through which SOUL passes to the God planes; the exit from the body for Soul at the time of DEATH; the third region, or STRATOSPHERE, which is filled with a brilliant light which extends for miles into the sky.

daya. *DAH-yah* Mercy; an act of giving to anyone who is unable to help himself.

Dayaka. *dah-YAH-kah* The LIVING ECK MASTER in LEMURIA.

Dayaka Temple. *dah-YAH-kah* TEMPLE OF GOLDEN WISDOM in the city of ARHIRIT on the ETHERIC PLANE. LAI TSI is the guardian of the SHARIYAT-KI-SUGMAD there.

Dayal. *DAH-yahl* The LIVING ECK MASTER, the MAHANTA; the act of being merciful, as the ECK MASTER always is to all SOULS and life-forms.

death. The translation from one body to another; the separation of the body and the vital astral force. At death, those SOULS following the path of ECKANKAR are taken by the LIVING ECK MASTER to whatever region of the INNER WORLDS they have earned; others not under the Living ECK Master are taken before the DHARAM RAYA, who administers karma according to their deeds.

Decates. *deh-KAH-tehz* The LIVING ECK MASTER of his time on the continent of ATLANTIS, in the city of SAR-KURTEVA.

dedication. Devotion to something sacred. The devotion of CHELAS to the ECK and the LIVING ECK MASTER. The greatest asset of a chela.

déjà vu. *DAY-jah VOO* The ability to know and see the past, and understand the future.

Delphi. *See* ORACLES.

D

desire. The thirst for material worldly things; feeling; comes from the love of objects of the senses; the offspring of the senses; the wanting of the senses which overwhelms the MIND and enslaves SOUL.

desireless life. *See* DETACHMENT; VAIRAG.

detachment. Giving up strong affection for the environment and possessions, but not ceasing to identify with them; becoming independent of them; mentally free from love of the world and all worldly DESIRES. *See* VAIRAG.

devas. *DAY-vahz* Male ANGELS, above ordinary men; they help serve man in many ways.

devil. The lower MIND, when not monitored by SOUL, begins to out-create It. Psychology calls it the SUBCONSCIOUS MIND, and Christianity says it is the devil; in ECK, it is the KAL NIRANJAN, who is the entity in charge of the negative forces.

devotee. One who is deeply devoted to the LIVING ECK MASTER or any Master. One who has great love for the teacher and devotion to him.

devotion. *See* DEDICATION.

devtas. *DEHV-tahz* A kind of ANGEL who serves mankind and is above ordinary man.

dham. *DAHM* A country or region in the other worlds.

dhamma. *DAH-mah* Doctrine or guiding principle accepted by the CHELA.

dhani. *DAH-nee* Ruler, or lord, of the inner spiritual regions.

Dharam Ray. *DAHR-ahm RAY* The negative power which controls the lower worlds; law and order; system; also designates religion or any religious system.

Dharam Raya. *DAHR-ahm RAY-ah* The righteous judge who sits enthroned to judge those who die or leave the PHYSICAL

PLANE, according to their deserts; the karma earned while in the physical worlds.

dharma. *DAHR-muh* The Law of Life; the righteousness of life; doing what is right; the code of conduct that sustains the right ethics in life.

dharmakaya. *DAHR-muh-KAH-yah* The recognition of the illusion and sport of the negative viewed as separate forms from the position of the fifth, or SOUL, PLANE; the viewing of the illusion from this position.

dharma megha. *DAHR-muh MAY-gah* A kind of SAMADHI, an absorption of the MIND into the object of CONTEMPLATION with complete DETACHMENT or VAIRAG.

Dhun. *DOON* HEAVENLY MUSIC; the melody of ECK; the BANI; DIVINE SPIRIT; the ESSENCE that gives life to all.

Dhunatmik. *doo-NAHT-mik* The true Word, or name, of the SUGMAD; VOICE OF THE SUGMAD, the Sound which cannot be spoken; It has no written symbol. *See also* VARNATMIK.

Dhyan. *DYAHN* The viewing of the LIVING ECK MASTER on the inner.

Dhyana. *DYAHN-nah* The CHELA's perfect vision of the Master on the inner, when the very sight of him inspires tremendous affection; the technique which brings about the meeting with the Master on the inner and the ability to travel with him to the higher worlds.

dialectics of ECKANKAR. The ability to talk about the works of ECKANKAR to anyone making inquiries into them.

diamond, month of the. *See* JOURNEY OF SOUL; MOKSHOVE.

dinta. *DEEN-tah* HUMILITY, the opposite of AHANKARA, VANITY.

Dionysus. *die-uh-NIS-uhs* A Greek master who was taught by the ADEPTS of ECKANKAR.

direct projection. One of the five kinds of SOUL TRAVEL techniques.

disciplines of ECK. SELF-DISCIPLINE, or control of the subjective self, is the only discipline suggested in ECKANKAR; can be gained by the study of the ECK works, putting the attention on the LIVING ECK MASTER, and doing a spiritual exercise at least once every day.

discourses of ECK. The personal and group studies of the outer, or physical, understanding of ECKANKAR.

discrimination. The recognition that there is no good nor evil, no beauty nor ugliness, no sin, and that these are concepts of the MIND, the DUAL FORCES in the matter worlds; the ability to make right judgments; to distinguish between those actions which contribute to spiritual growth and those which are a waste of time. *See* VIVEKA.

disintegration. One of the three characteristics of the human state of being in the PHYSICAL BODY of man.

divine cause. *See* ECK.

divine consciousness. A state of God-knowing.

divine Creator. *See* SUGMAD.

divine ECK. *See* ECK.

divine energy. The forming faculty of the ECK POWER which brings about the orderly, wider growth and fuller expression which develops out of former experiences; the power for the movement of divine spiritual operation, which uses each individual as Its CHANNEL, according to the state of CONSCIOUSNESS.

divine essence. Antecedent cause; first cause; the OVERSOUL, God. *See also* SUGMAD.

divine faculty. The IMAGINATION; the inner action, DESIRE, picturing, expecting.

D

divine force. Life; conscious Self; the source of INTELLIGENCE; expressing as LIFE-FORCE and intelligence.

divine flow. The movement of SPIRIT as It moves out from the GODHEAD, the OCEAN OF LOVE AND MERCY, and returns, carrying with It the CONSCIOUSNESS of Itself and all Its forms; the centripetal and centrifugal flow of the ECK.

divine grace. The SUGMAD; that which is not limited by the conditions of ability, but conditions ability; that in which all things live, move, and have their BEING; the granting by the Supreme Being of all BEINGNESS.

divine ideal. The divine ECK; to the extent that the mirror of CONSCIOUSNESS blurs or clearly reflects the image of divine ideal, there arises a corresponding feeble or vigorous reproduction in external life.

divine knowledge. The knowledge that SOUL can do no wrong; the knowledge of BEING; of the good of the SUGMAD.

divine law. Everything that exists is some MANIFESTATION of the ECK POWER from which and by which all things have been created and are continually being recreated. SOUL is the greatest achievement of CREATION; It exists throughout ETERNITY, loves and seeks Its CREATOR, and will attain the highest glory.

divine love. The merciful love with which the SUGMAD looks upon all CREATION; the OCEAN OF LOVE AND MERCY; the SUGMAD.

divine power. That which flows out of the universal body of the SUGMAD to sustain all the worlds; the LIGHT AND SOUND; the ECK.

divine purpose. The continual enlightening of man for his spiritual evolution and unfoldment by TRUTH, or SPIRIT.

divine reality. The GODHEAD; the fountain of POWER behind all apparent cause; the all-embracing unity from which nothing can be separated.

divine rights. The righteous law. *See also* DANDA.

divine Self. The divine nature of man, SOUL; SPIRIT; that which lifts man to the heights of glory, POWER, and splendor.

divine source. *See* DIVINE REALITY.

D

divine spark. The inner ESSENCE, the divinity which is of the SUGMAD; the founding master of a religion or movement; the polarity between the followers and God.

divine Spirit. The Voice, that ESSENCE; the Holy Ghost, the Comforter that gives life to all; the ECK. *See also* DIVINE POWER; ECK.

divine truth. The one and unchanging SPIRIT; separation or a divided state of the SUGMAD is illusion; the oneness of the SUGMAD.

divine Voice. The all-creative ECK out of which all other sounds arise. *See also* DHUNATMIK.

divine will. Absolute will; the will or DESIRE of the SUGMAD; those principles or laws of the SUGMAD, which when abided by, lead to SPIRITUAL UNFOLDMENT. The will of the ECK, or positive, power as opposed to the will of the negative, or KAL, power.

divine wisdom. That WISDOM beyond the wisdom that life in the lower worlds can furnish; wisdom gained through inner ENLIGHTENMENT; the quality of being wise beyond the abilities of the senses or the MIND.

doctrine of cycles. Based upon the fundamental principle in the psychic philosophy, which is: as above, so below.

doctrine of numbers. Numbers are symbols of DIVINE REALITIES; a key to the ancient views on life.

doctrine of reincarnation. The 999 cycles of INCARNATIONS on the earth planet which form the one MAJOR CYCLE of evolutionary life toward perfection.

dodal chakra. *doh-DAHL CHAH-krah* The CHAKRA behind the eyes; the sixth chakra; the seat of SOUL in the waking state; the

THIRD EYE, the TISRA TIL; ruled by the MIND element; also called the Do-dal-Kanwal.

Do-dal-Kanwal. *See* DODAL CHAKRA.

door of Soul. The TISRA TIL, the THIRD EYE; the opening through which SOUL passes into the INNER WORLDS.

Doreti. *doh-RAY-tee* The third twelve-year cycle of the DUODENARY CYCLE; the Years of the Brilliant Sun. *See also* CYCLES OF TWELVE.

dream consciousness. The psychic states of CONSCIOUSNESS.

Dream Master. The MAHANTA, the LIVING ECK MASTER.

dreams. One of three states of CONSCIOUSNESS of man; the other two are waking and sleeping; the unconscious MIND's way of satisfying its secret and hidden wishes.

dream state. AWARENESS on the level of emotion, the ASTRAL PLANE; the realization of all perceptions in the ASTRAL WORLD; used by the ECK MASTERS to help the CHELAS work off KARMIC PATTERNS.

dream teachings. Given in the first stages of ECK at the TEMPLES OF GOLDEN WISDOM by the Vairagi Masters, to assist the NEOPHYTE in his SPIRITUAL UNFOLDMENT.

dream techniques. Techniques for SOUL TRAVEL used in ECKANKAR; given in the *ECK Dream Discourses*.

dream travel. Travel in the DREAM STATE, the first step to SOUL TRAVEL.

drugs. A mask that obstructs the true way to God; an artificial, destructive means of escape from the trials and tribulations of life and the physical worlds.

dual consciousness. AWARENESS of the physical state while being in the SOUL state during SOUL TRAVEL.

dual forces. The negative, or KAL NIRANJAN, at one pole and the positive, or ECK, at the other.

dual worlds. The worlds of matter, energy, time, and space; of negative and positive; of isness and not-isness; male and female. All the worlds below the Fifth Plane: the PHYSICAL, ASTRAL, CAUSAL, MENTAL, and ETHERIC PLANES.

D

dukkha. *DOOK-kah* Suffering or illness.

duodenary cycle. The GREATER CYCLE, or cycle of 144 years; also called the HARAM; rotation into higher VIBRATIONS which affects men, nations, and planets. *See* CYCLES OF TWELVE.

dutas. *DOO-tahz* Messengers of YAMA, the KING OF THE DEAD; ANGELS OF DEATH, or the dark ANGELS, as they are called by the Christians.

Dvadach-dal-Kanwal. *See* HRIDA CHAKRA.

Dwapara Yuga. *dwah-PAH-rah YOO-gah* Third of the four cycles of ages, the COPPER AGE, which endures 864,000 years and precedes the last age, the KALI YUGA. In it the forces of light and darkness, good and evil, pleasure and pain are equally balanced.

dying daily. Leaving the body at will for SOUL TRAVEL; coming and going at will between the physical and the higher worlds through the SOUL POWER; dying while still living, the daily routine of ECK travelers.

dynamic energy. The SOUND CURRENT; the DIVINE ENERGY; the ECK; the AUDIBLE LIFE STREAM stepped down to meet material conditions. *See also* DIVINE POWER.

Dzyani. *DZYAH-nee* September, THE MONTH OF THE AGATE, the days of friendship, according to the ancient ECK-VIDYA measurements of time. The journey of high success, POWER, achievements, and splendor. *See also* JOURNEY OF SOUL.

E

E

Eagle-eyed Adepts. *See* ADEPT(S); VAIRAGI ADEPTS.

Ebkia. *EHB-kee-yah* The fourth month of the ECK-VIDYA calendar, April, called the days of hope, the month of the opal. This JOURNEY OF SOUL is the primary search for peace.

ECK. *EHK* The AUDIBLE LIFE CURRENT; all that is life; the eternal truth and eternal paradox within all; encompasses all the teachings of religions and philosophies; stream of LIFE-FORCE; the science of TOTAL AWARENESS that grows out of the experiences of SOUL TRAVEL; the realization of GOD CONSCIOUSNESS; the thread that binds together all beings in all planes, all universes, throughout all time, and beyond all time into ETERNITY; Life-force, self-consciousness; the HOLY SPIRIT; the source of all; the CREATOR of all things; the great forming force which works in a creative way; the constructive forming force; is everywhere; the ESSENCE of the SUGMAD; the science of GOD-REALIZATION. *See also* DIVINE POWER; DIVINE SPIRIT.

ECK Adepts. *See* ADEPTS; ECK MASTERS; VAIRAGI ADEPTS.

ECKANKAR. *EHK-ahn-kahr* The path of TOTAL AWARENESS; the way of all things; means "CO-WORKER with God"; a teaching that gives knowledge of both the LIGHT and the Sound which contains the total sum of all teaching emanating from God; the very foundation of all systems of science, and the key to success in unfolding all spiritual powers; the Ancient Science of SOUL TRAVEL. Projection of the inner CONSCIOUSNESS, which travels through the lower states until it ascends into the ecstatic states where the subject feels he possesses an AWARENESS of the religious experience of BEING; achieved through a series of spiritual exercises known only to the followers of this science.

ECKANKAR, goals of. Serenity, poise, and an organized will from the objective viewpoint, and the CHANNEL for the ECK POWER on the subjective side; to reach SELF- and GOD-REALIZATION.

ECKANKAR, thirty-two facets of. Thirty-two varied phases of SPIRITUAL UNFOLDMENT to be found on the path of ECKANKAR.

ECK, basic principle of. The LIGHT and the Sound, the ESSENCE of the SUGMAD.

ECK chela. Student, disciple, or follower of ECKANKAR; the second step on this path. *See* ACOLYTE.

ECK creeds, ancient. (1) Perfection has no limitation, nor is it temporary or changeable, while pleasure and suffering are the conditions of material existence; (2) all life flows from the SUGMAD, downward into the worlds below and through them, and nothing can exist without this COSMIC CURRENT known as ECK, which can be heard as Sound and seen as LIGHT. Therefore it is necessary for man to always be aware of the sounds of the ECK and see the NURI, or LIGHT BODY of the SUGMAD in order to live within the highest spiritual realms.

ECK Current. *See* CURRENT.

ECK Dhun. *See* DHUN.

ECK doctrine. The principles and teachings of the path of ECKANKAR.

ECK exercises. Spiritual, or contemplative, exercises used by ECK CHELAS to unfold their spiritual CONSCIOUSNESS; given in the books and DISCOURSES of ECKANKAR.

ECK force. The principle factor, the prime action in the whole CREATION; the life and SOUL of everything; that which produces a sharp reaction when It comes in contact with matter; that which motivates every activity in the universe; the all in all. *See also* DIVINE POWER; DIVINE SPIRIT; ECK; ECK POWER.

ECK initiate. *See* INITIATE.

ECK Initiator. A HIGHER INITIATE of ECKANKAR who has been appointed by the LIVING ECK MASTER to perform INITIATIONS.

ECKist. *EHK-ist* A follower, or disciple, of ECKANKAR; one who spreads the message of ECKANKAR; a CHELA of the LIVING ECK MASTER, who works in accordance with the laws of ECKANKAR.

ECK Kalam. *EHK kah-LAHM* The ECK Sound; the HEAVENLY MUSIC; one of the SPIRITUAL EXERCISES OF ECK.

ECK, Law of. The CHELA or student in a human body must have a Master in the human body.

ECK, living. Central life-giving energy generated on all planes, the plane of the above, beyond, and below; the indwelling LIFE-FORCE on all planes, which is also the planes themselves.

ECK Marg. *EHK MAHRG* The path to the SUGMAD; the path of ECKANKAR; the secret path of the SOUND CURRENT.

ECK Master, Living. *See* LIVING ECK MASTER.

ECK Masters. The ADEPTS of the Vairagi; the true SPIRITUAL MASTERS who have reached the state of CONSCIOUSNESS of relative perfection; the teachers and guides for the path of ECKANKAR through all the planes of the lower worlds. Lords of life and DEATH. *See also* ADEPTS; LIVING ECK MASTER; MAHANTA; VAIRAGI ADEPTS.

ECK-nida region. *EHK-NEE-dah* That area of the ATMA, or SOUL, PLANE where the records of the INITIATES of the Seventh through Twelfth planes are kept.

ECK path. *See* ECK MARG.

ECK power. That INTELLIGENCE which sustains all life within the cosmic worlds; the force of love; the only power of the true nature of the SUGMAD; above the dichotomy of good and evil; the love CURRENT which is always moving into the worlds of matter, energy, time, and space. *See also* DIVINE POWER; DIVINE SPIRIT; ECK FORCE.

ECK rays. Three main rays or forces (light, energy) which are sent out to the lower worlds: the WISDOM force, the power force, and the freedom force. From these indirect MANIFESTATIONS of the force of the SUGMAD flow offshoots which bring the number of rays to ten. They are simply beams which are offshoots of the spiritual form, the ECK, the first manifestation of the SUGMAD in the SOUL, or Fifth, PLANE.

ECK saints. The SPIRITUAL TRAVELERS, the ADEPTS of the Vairagi, the ECK MASTERS; a mysterious race of people who give teachings to those who can understand. *See also* VAIRAGI ADEPTS.

ECK Satsang. *EHK SAHT-sahng* CHELAS of ECKANKAR gathered together to read, hear, and study the works of ECK. Acts as a unitized CHANNEL for the ECK FORCE, or power, forming the TRINITY OF ECKANKAR with the LIVING ECK MASTER and the ECK (the SOUND CURRENT).

ECKshar. *EHK-shahr* The state of SELF-REALIZATION, which precedes GOD CONSCIOUSNESS; the ENLIGHTENMENT of the LIGHT AND SOUND through the path of ECKANKAR; MOKSHA.

ECK Sound Current. *See* DIVINE POWER; DIVINE SPIRIT; ECK; SOUND CURRENT.

ECK Spirit. The WORD; that which sustains and originates the whole CREATION which man, plant, creature, or mineral feels, sees, or observes. *See also* CURRENT; DIVINE POWER; DIVINE SPIRIT; ECK; SOUND CURRENT.

ECK Spiritual Aide. Also ESA. HIGHER INITIATES in ECK who serve as vehicles for SPIRIT and listening posts for people who want someone to listen to their spiritual problems.

ECK Spiritual Council. INITIATES of the Eighth Circle in ECKANKAR who are appointed by the LIVING ECK MASTER to serve as an advisory council to him and as ambassadors of ECK.

ECK Traveler. The AGENT OF GOD, the representative of the spiritual LIGHT, the COSMIC LIGHT of Itself; truth within itself; man manifested in whom individualism and universalism are combined in their full expression, who stands alone, is a law unto himself, and is a citizen of the whole world. *See also* ECK MASTERS; LIVING ECK MASTER.

E

ECK Vahana. *EHK vah-HAH-nah*   *See* VAHANA; VAHANA MARG.

ECK-Vidya. *EHK-VEE-dyah* The ancient science of prophecy; the modus operandi of delving into the past, present, and future used by the ADEPTS of the Ancient Order of Vairagi; an aspect of ECK, the FULFILLMENT of the TOTAL AWARENESS of God.

ECK Word. Manifests in the LIVING ECK MASTER as the WORD or the embodiment of the Sound; the ECK.

ECK-Ynari. *EHK-yi-NAH-ree* A facet of ECKANKAR used by the ECK MASTERS as a way of understanding the UNCONSCIOUS; the most ancient means used to judge the DREAM STATE; the secret knowledge of DREAMS.

ECK Youth Council ECK youth up to the age of twenty-five who are appointed by the LIVING ECK MASTER to serve as an advisory council to him and as ambassadors to the youth of ECK.

Ede. *EH-deh* First female; the companion of ADOM, the Rabi, the first man.

ego. The realization of one's self as a HUMAN CONSCIOUSNESS; the personality, which when we rise above it, we become the individual; the mental self, the I.

EK. *EHK* Modern form of "Ecstasies" or "ek-marg," used to describe both the result and the techniques of EXTERIORIZATION. Known to the pagan Greeks, and to the Romans (as "superstitio"), the practice consisted in reaching, through concentration, a mystic state in which the subject believed his spirit to have left his body. BUDDHISM fostered similar techniques through MEDITATION.

In the modern Western world, the practice was revived in midtwentieth century by the American savant Paul Twitchell, who set forth a number of methods for leaving the body, with the object of achieving TOTAL AWARENESS of the divine ground of Divine Being.

ekacitta. *ehk-ah-SEE-tah* One moment beyond time and space; the experience of being out of the physical state of CONSCIOUSNESS.

ekaggata. *ehk-ah-GAH-tah* Being one-pointed in thought; single-minded.

ekam adwaitam. *EH-kahm ah-DWIE-tahm* The one second in ETERNITY experienced by those who seek God.

elementals. At the bottom of the SPIRITUAL HIERARCHY are the four elementals: gnomes, salamanders, undines, and sylphs. Gnomes, the earth creatures, are in charge of the earth elements—gold, silver, other minerals, etc. Next are the salamanders, the fire elementals, which live in the fire and look like small lizards or dragons and take care of the fire—sometimes destructively, sometimes for the good of man. The undines, which are the water spirits, the mermaids of legends, live in the world of water and take care of that element. Last are the sylphs, the air spirits, known in fables as fairies, which control the air elements. They look like graceful, young women and are gentle until they are disturbed or become angry; storms are the result of their rages.

Eleusinian Mystery School. *ehl-yoo-SIN-yehn* An ancient ECK school which taught how to reach the divine GODHEAD.

Elohim. *See* YAHVEH.

emanative sphere. A circle, or disc, of rays invisible to the outer senses but perceptible to the INNER VISION, which are the thoughts and feelings of each person's particular universe surrounding the body. *See also* AURA.

embodiment of God. Each SOUL which is the living truth.

emerald. *See* ASTIK; JOURNEY OF SOUL.

Emotional body. The ASTRAL sheath, or BODY, through which SOUL experiences the ASTRAL PLANE.

Endless Plane. ALAYA LOK; the Seventh Plane; ETERNITY seems to begin and end here; the word is HUM, and the sound is of deep humming.

E

enlightenment. GOD-REALIZATION; the stage of ultimate truth; the state of knowledge of the ULTIMATE REALITY; the awakened state; becoming aware of God; the breakthrough into the states of no time or space; GOD-CONSCIOUSNESS.

Epictetus. *ehp-ik-TEHT-uhs* A Greek stoic philosopher who taught ECK in Rome during the first century A.D., and was one of the Masters of the Ancient Order of the VAIRAGI ADEPTS.

Erutua. *ehr-oo-TOO-ah* The ninth twelve-year cycle in the DUODE-NARY CYCLE of the ECK-VIDYA; the Years of the Abundant Fruits. *See also* CYCLES OF TWELVE.

Eshwar-Khanewale. *EHSH-wahr-KAH-neh-wahl* The ADEPTS who live in the spiritual city of AGAM DES; the God-eaters, who partake of cosmic energy instead of material food and live to great ages beyond the normal span of human life.

esoteric. The secret knowledge not obtainable by the uninitiated; the opposite of EXOTERIC.

essence. The DIVINE VOICE of the SUGMAD; that which gives life to all; the PRIMAL WORD; the all-creative ECK; the WORD, or BANI; the true element of the LIFE-FORCE, the little atoms which spin within us. *See* DIVINE POWER; DIVINE SPIRIT; ECK.

essence of Spirit. Nobility, aesthetics, life, love, beauty, and the single primary impulse to express truth, and the love and beauty It feels Itself to be; the breath of God.

Essenes. *ehs-EENZ* A mystical group of masters who were trained as ECK teachers and acted as part of the mystery school of wisdom for the purpose of spreading the truth of the SUGMAD. *See also* ZADOK.

E

eternity. All is eternity; an expression of life without a sense of time and space, already established by the SUGMAD; the DIVINE CONSCIOUSNESS; the present is always eternity, and SOUL is always in the present.

Etheric body. The higher portion of the MENTAL BODY; the impressional self, the sanskara body which contains the SANSKARAS, the impressions of all former lives in a different way than the CAUSAL BODY.

etheric mind. The top half of the first sheath wrapped around SOUL as It descends into the lower worlds; the SUBCONSCIOUS or impressional MIND; the BUDDHI SHARIR which lies between the MENTAL BODY and Soul; transmitter of impressions between the Mental body and Soul, and Soul and the Mental body. *See also* ETHERIC BODY.

Etheric Plane. The top of the MENTAL PLANE, the UNCONSCIOUS plane sometimes called the SUBCONSCIOUS; the source of primitive thought; the very thin sheath between the MENTAL BODY and the ATMA SARUP, the SOUL BODY.

etheric vibrations. The movement of everything that is static, as SPIRIT, when set in motion by the moving in and vibrating through infinite space, not only of the Voice of God, but of God ITSELF; that Word which can be heard by the INNER EAR which has been trained to hear It.

Ethics, Law of. That which is not selfish, which is good for the whole, which will not harm one, and will do justice for all concerned; actions for the benefit of all.

Evolution, Law of. Establishes inequality in all things and beings and their continued effort for SPIRITUAL UNFOLDMENT.

exoteric. That teaching which is revealed to the physical eyes and ears; suitable for the uninitiated or outsiders; the opposite of ESOTERIC.

exteriorization. That action, or experience, by SOUL of being elsewhere than the physical body; being out of the PHYSICAL BODY as

AWARENESS or knowing; being aware without using the body's senses. *See also* ASTRAL PROJECTION; SOUL TRAVEL.

extrasensory perception. ESP; the moving of MIND and thoughts beyond self, and the recognition of happenings between self and others, or outside the self environment; one of the THIRTY-TWO FACETS OF ECKANKAR.

Eye, Spiritual. *See* TISRA TIL.

E

F

faces of the Master. *See* TWO FACES OF THE MASTER.

Facsimiles, Law of. The sixth law of the physical universe, that all effects in life are brought about by the thoughts and pictures in the MIND of the individual. *See also* LAWS OF THE PHYSICAL UNIVERSE.

faculties of mind. *See* MIND, FACULTIES OF.

faith. The keystone of all spiritual life; belief and total acceptance of the SUGMAD and the MAHANTA, the LIVING ECK MASTER as ITS agent; to act as if one is; belief in the WORD, the ECK, the LIGHT and the Sound; confidence in the Master and what he represents spiritually, and confidence in his spiritual works as the way of God.

false prophets. Those who claim mastership, but who are not in a long line of Masters who have existed in the past, and have not had the spiritual mantle handed down to them by a predecessor from a distinct line of spiritual hierarchy.

fantasy, realm of. The area which many seekers of God fall into when trying to travel the spiritual path alone.

Faqiti Monastery. *fah-KEE-tee* The TEMPLE OF GOLDEN WISDOM on the ASURATI LOK, or Desert world, in the Gobi Desert.

Farank. *FAH-rahnk* The fifth twelve-year cycle in the DUODENARY CYCLE called the Years of the Full Moon. *See also* CYCLES OF TWELVE.

F

Far Country, the. The vast world lying beyond the earth plane; a series of spiritual universes which can be experienced by SOUL.

fasting. Going without food for periods of time; in ECKANKAR, the day of fasting is Friday and is part of the practice of SELF-DISCIPLINE.

fate karma. *See* PRAABDH KARMA.

Fattura Della Morte. *fah-TOO-rah DEH-lah MOR-teh* The death-maker; one who can bring DEATH to another at his own DESIRE.

fear. A state of MIND arising out of the psychic CONSCIOUSNESS; an emotion which inhibits and poisons the consciousness of man along with ANGER, worry, sentimental emotionalism, and envy, as a way of preventing SPIRITUAL UNFOLDMENT.

feminine principle. The passive, negative, or receptive aspect of the energies of God; the universal mother principle in the HUMAN CONSCIOUSNESS; puts together the organizations and social elements of life and holds them together; sees, invents, and devises the means to keep the social structure together.

Fifth Initiation. The first of the true INITIATIONS; the MAHDIS, the BROTHERS OF THE LEAF; CO-WORKERS with the MAHANTA, the LIVING ECK MASTER; the initiation of the FIFTH PLANE.

Firdusi. *feer-DOO-see* A great Persian poet during the eleventh century.

First Grand Division. In literature referring to two grand divisions, the First Grand Division is the planes of the lower worlds.

five passions of the mind. KAMA (LUST); KRODHA (ANGER); LOBHA (GREED); MOHA (ATTACHMENT); and AHANKARA (VANITY). *See also* MIND.

five virtues. VIVEKA (DISCRIMINATION); KSHAMA (forgiveness, tolerance); SANTOSHA (contentment); VAIRAG (DETACHMENT); DINTA (HUMILITY).

fountainhead, divine. The SUGMAD, God; that from which all else springs; ECK, the fountainhead from which springs all religions and philosophies.

Freedom Ray. The third of the ten forces, or rays, of the ECK which are sent out to the worlds below by the SUGMAD through the ECK.

freedom, spiritual. See SPIRITUAL FREEDOM.

F

free will. The power and right each SOUL has to decide whether to follow the way of the KAL, or negative, or to follow the path of ECKANKAR.

Freticrets. *FREHT-i-krehts* The last race before the end of the KALI YUGA, or Iron Age who will be dealers in black MAGIC; a desperate and ruthless race from the world of Pluto; they will control the earth and most of the planets throughout the universe.

Fubbi Quantz. *FOO-bee KWONTS* The LIVING ECK MASTER during the time of BUDDHA, about 500 B.C. He completed his mission, then immortalized his body, and is now the guardian of the SHARIYAT-KI-SUGMAD at the KATSUPARI MONASTERY in northern Tibet. A teacher of FIRDUSI, the Persian poet, he was also the spiritual guide for Columbus and encouraged his voyage to the Americas in order to revitalize the depleted nutrition of the Europeans.

fulfillment. Acting out the wish as though already fulfilled.

functions of life. The two main functions of life are: (1) God as SPIRIT is eternal, everywhere, and unchanging; and (2) prayers by the millions have been answered down through the ages. What has been true of God in the past is true now; if true for some, it is true for all.

future karma. See KARMA, LAW OF; SINCHIT KARMA.

G

Gakko. *GAHK-koh* A state of relative perfection within the ATMA LOK (the world of SOUL) where all or most of the ECK MASTERS live who are not doing duty in the other planes and worlds; the world of BEING, a state of CONSCIOUSNESS. Name of first ECK Master.

gakko nibbana. *GAHK-koh NEE-bah-nah* The dying away of the constituents of empirical existence, which is the entering of SOUL into the world of BEING. *See also* KINSLO NIBBANA; NIBBUTA.

Gandharuas. *gahn-dah-ROO-ahz* The heavenly musicians, especially those on the ASTRAL PLANE, whose music, when heard, seems to be that of the ECK life stream.

Ganesh. *gah-NEHSH* An agent of the SUGMAD serving mankind and helping to carry on the administration of the physical universe, who stands practically at the foot of the list of subordinates in the GRAND HIERARCHY; a CURRENT, god, or power of the working force of the universe; lord of the first ASTRAL PLANE; king of the lower world; the lowest part of the body, the GUDA CHAKRA.

Gare-Hira. *GAH-ray-HEE-rah* The TEMPLE OF GOLDEN WISDOM located in the spiritual city of AGAM DES, home of the ESHWAR-KHANEWALE, the God-eaters. YAUBL SACABI is the guardian of the second section of the SHARIYAT-KI-SUGMAD here.

Garvata. *gahr-VAH-tah* The third month of the ECK-VIDYA calendar, March, the month of the jade, the days of joy. During this journey, SOUL is restless and has a great sense of urgency. *See also* JOURNEY OF SOUL.

G

gatha. *GAH-thah* Set of religious verses, set down by those who have had flashes of spiritual insight.

Gathas. *GAH-thahz* Oldest part of the Avesta, the religious book of those who follow ZOROASTER, the Persian sage who lived about 600 B.C; supposed to be an authentic version of his teachings.

gaze of the Master. *See* TIWAJA.

generic principle, ECK. The first positive factor in the whole CREATION is SPIRIT—the invisible power which concentrates the primordial ether into forms and endows those forms with various modes of motion; the primary positive factor is the feeling and thought of the universal spirit of HU. *See also* PRINCIPLE OF HU.

Geshe. *GEHSH-ay* A Tibetan title meaning Doctor of Divinity.

Geutan. *geh-OO-tahn* The third great ECK MASTER who served the people of LEMURIA and warned them of the coming destruction of their continent.

ghata. *GAH-tah* Act of opening the CONSCIOUSNESS; sometimes called SATORI, or ENLIGHTENMENT.

Giana. *gee-AH-nah* A word chanted in the spiritual exercise, the UNMANI DHUN.

Giani. *gee-AH-nee* A learned CHELA; one who practices or walks the path of WISDOM.

Giani Marg. *gee-AH-nee MAHRG* The path of ESOTERIC wisdom; the path of studying at the TEMPLES OF GOLDEN WISDOM.

Ginthe. *GIN-theh* The second twelve-year cycle in the DUODENARY CYCLE; the Years of the Bright Snows. *See also* CYCLES OF TWELVE.

Gita. *GEE-tah* Also Geeta. A book of Indian religious philosophy.

gnata. *GNAH-tah* The knower of God.

gnomes. *See* ELEMENTALS.

Gnothe Seauton. *guh-NOH-theh seh-ah-OO-tahn* "Know thyself"; this is written over the doors of ancient temples, that man's first duty is to know himself.

God. *See* SUGMAD.

God Consciousness. Levels of CONSCIOUSNESS beyond the margin of attention; the MANIFESTATION of spiritual energy, ECK POWER, made up of atoms in space; God Awareness, that which lies beyond the physical consciousness; GOD-REALIZATION, full AWARENESS of identity with God; complete and conscious awareness of God.

God-Consciousness Plane. The HUKIKAT LOK, the fourth world of the God Worlds, or the EIGHTH PLANE of CONSCIOUSNESS.

God-eaters. *See* ESHWAR-KHANEWALE.

God freedom. The perfect freedom to make decisions out of one's own state of CONSCIOUSNESS.

Godhead. The DIVINE REALITY, a fountain of power back of all apparent cause. *See* FOUNTAINHEAD, DIVINE; PRINCIPLES OF THE GODHEAD.

Godhood. That state of BEINGNESS which is the AWARENESS that SOUL has of Its Godlike self, which It already is.

God-knowledge. *See* GOD-REALIZATION; PRADA VIDYA.

God, Law of. Everything has its origin in SPIRIT; DIVINE TRUTH is one and unchanging.

Godman. The spiritual leader of ECKANKAR; he has attained the highest state of CONSCIOUSNESS known to mankind.

God power. *See* DIVINE ENERGY; DIVINE POWER; DIVINE SPIRIT; ECK.

God-Realization. Void, omnipresent, silent, pure, and strangely peaceful; cannot be apprehended with the physical senses; realization or AWARENESS of the God State, the knowledge of God; attainment of the higher spiritual state of the supernatural life;

the uniting of the human and the divine natures. *See also* GOD CONSCIOUSNESS.

God seekers. Those who search for the realization of God, not knowing that it is always with them.

Gods of Eternity. The nine unknown gods who watch over and guard the golden scripts of the SUGMAD; the keepers of the divine flame of WISDOM.

God Vidya. *See* GOD CONSCIOUSNESS; PRADA VIDYA.

God Worlds of ECK. *See* SPIRITUAL WORLDS.

Golden Age. *See* SATYA YUGA.

Golden Heart. The loving heart, the open heart. The Golden Heart is full of the love for God and has COMPASSION for those who are lost in the darkness of the HUMAN CONSCIOUSNESS.

Golden Wisdom Temple. *See* TEMPLES OF GOLDEN WISDOM.

Golden-tongued Wisdom. A form of the ECK-VIDYA, the Ancient Science of Prophecy. The ECK-Vidya generally covers the past, present, and future of an individual, a nation, or the universe as a whole; whereas the Golden-tongued Wisdom focuses more on the individual and his relationship with his immediate environment. It can come as a nudge, a direct message from the INNER MASTER, a dream, or a WAKING DREAM.

Gopal Das. *GOH-pahl DAHS* The LIVING ECK MASTER in Egypt, 3000 B.C., who founded the mystery cults of OSIRIS and Isis; the guardian of the fourth section of the SHARIYAT-KI-SUGMAD on the ASTRAL PLANE; he teaches at the TEMPLE OF GOLDEN WISDOM there.

Gotta. *GOH-tah* One of the first ECK MASTERS of the Ancient Order of the VAIRAGI ADEPTS.

Grace, Law of. To be in accord with the ways of the SUGMAD for making each a divine CHANNEL, through working in the area of nonattachment mainly through discipline of the emotions.

Grand Hierarchy. The galaxy of lords, rulers, CREATORS, and gover-
nors of all the heavenly spheres; in every subdivision of each of
the grand divisions there is a ruler or governor; each has been
appointed by the Supreme One to discharge the duties of his
particular region.

grand paradox. SOUL lives forever by giving, not by receiving.

greater cycle. The HARAM, or DUODENARY CYCLE of 144 years; higher
VIBRATIONS which rotate every twelfth year to uplift SOULS. *See
also* CYCLES OF TWELVE.

G

greed. One of the FIVE PASSIONS OF THE MIND; called LOBHA.

group Soul. A number of SOULS, like a family or a community, tied
together by a common cause; an entity in which the members
act and react upon one another as they unfold spiritually.

guda chakra. *See* MULCHAKRA.

guna(s). *GOO-nah(z)* From the yoga of Patanjali; the three basic
attributes of the Universal Mind Power, the KAL force. They are
SATTVA (light); RAJAS (creativity of motion); and TAMAS (darkness).

gupta vidya. *GOOP-tah VEE-dyah* ESOTERIC wisdom.

guru. *GOO-roo* The ordinary title for any teacher of spiritual
works.

Gurumukh. *GOO-roo-mook* One whose face is always turned to
the Master; a spiritual DEVOTEE. *See also* MANMUKH.

Gyanee. *gie-YAH-nee* An INITIATE of the Eighth Circle.

gyatri. *gie-YAH-tree* The word of power, the magic word sought
by all inner cults; the two-edged sword which can create or
destroy.

H

Habu Medinet. *HAH-boo mehd-ee-NEHT* The LIVING ECK MASTER in Persia around 490 B.C.

Hadjis. *HAHD-jeez* Books of the SHARIYAT-KI-SUGMAD.

Hafiz. *hah-FEEZ* Famous fourteenth-century poet of Persia who was a follower of ECK.

hak. *HAHK* A word designating truth, reality.

Hamsa. *HAHM-sah* An image of God as the divine bird which lays the world in the form of an egg; also may be Sa-ham, or "I am that"; SOUL.

Hansa. *HAHN-sah* A swan, or mythical bird of beauty, which symbolizes SOUL after It has reached the ATMA, or Fifth, PLANE.

Hansni Tunnel. *HAHN-snee* A tunnel of darkness through which those traveling the road to God pass between the MENTAL and ETHERIC planes.

Haqiqat. *hah-kee-KAHT* One of the four developments of man as recognized by the ECK MASTERS; the merging into truth and full realization of God.

haram. *See* CYCLES OF TWELVE, DUODENARY CYCLE; GREATER CYCLE.

Hari Ray. *HAH-ree RAY* A name for God (the SUGMAD).

Hari Tita. *HAH-ree TEE-tah* The Living ECK Master during the Trojan period of Greek history; he now works in the Alakh Lok, the sixth plane.

Harji. *HAYR-jee* A title of love and respect for Sri Harold Klemp. *See also* Klemp, Harold; Wah Z.

Harmonics, Law of. *See* Vibrations, Law of.

harmony. A principle of ECKANKAR, which is the perception that the "I AM" is ONE, always in harmony with ITSELF, including all things because there is no second Creative Power; total acceptance and oneness with.

Harold Klemp. *See* Klemp, Harold.

Hatha Yoga. *HAH-thah YOH-gah* A system of yoga which aims at the control of the MIND and the acquiring of psychic powers. Not needed by the ECK traveler.

hatred. One of the twin negative emotions which comes out of the stream of thought consciousness (the psychic, or lower-world, consciousness); the other emotion is fear.

Haurvatat. *hah-oor-VAH-taht* The fifth ray of light or way that the SUGMAD has to make ITSELF known to man; absolute, wholeness, perfection, and spirituality. *See also* Amesha Spentas.

heart center. The solar plexus; the point at which the part meets with the whole, the finite becomes the infinite, the uncreated becomes the created, the universal becomes individualized, and the invisible becomes visible; in yoga, the anahag chakra.

heavenly kingdom. The Ocean of Love and Mercy; the SUGMAD.

heavenly music. The primal Sound, the ECK; the Voice of the SUGMAD, the Dhunatmik; cannot be spoken or written; the original music, the heavenly white sound; the Word of the worlds.

heavenly worlds. The worlds of the SUGMAD; beyond matter, space, time, and energy.

hell.   A part of the lower world just above the physical in one corner of the ASTRAL WORLD; a mockup by the citizens of the earth world, manifested by religions to control their members through the priests.

Heraclians.   *heh-rah-KLEE-ahnz*   The tenth race to conquer and control the world; fair and just, they will rule around the year 6025 A.D., and the civilization will last from five hundred to one thousand years.

hereness of the SUGMAD.   The present state of life; part of the SUGMAD TRINITY.

H

Hiafi.   *hee-AH-fee*   The eleventh twelve-year cycle of the DUODENARY CYCLE called the Years of the Lavish Grains. *See also* CYCLES OF TWELVE.

hierarchy.   *See* GRAND HIERARCHY; SPIRITUAL HIERARCHY.

Higher Initiate.   Those of the Fifth Circle or above in ECKANKAR.

Himalayas.   *him-ah-LAY-ehz*   The highest known mountain system, lies between India and Tibet.

Himinbjor.   *HEEM-een-byohr*   A sacred mountain in the mythology of the German people.

Hindu Kush.   *HIN-doo KOOSH*   Mountain range along the border of northern Afghanistan and Pakistan, to the west of the HIMA-LAYAS. AGAM DES, TIRICH MIR, and REBAZAR TARZS's hut are all in the Hindu Kush.

Hipolito Fayolle.   *hee-POH-lee-toh fay-OHL*   The LIVING ECK MASTER during the eighteenth century, who lived to the age of ninety-seven and now works on the ALAKH LOK, the sixth plane.

Hittites.   *HIT-tiets*   The people who existed during the DWAPARA YUGA, or the COPPER AGE, who used copper for making weapons and were among the first to make the sword; among the first known conquerors in the history of mankind.

holy fire.   The holy fire of ECK. The love of all because it is life, and life is God; the spirit of the ECK; the burning love for all things, all people, and all life.

holy immortals. *See* AMESHA SPENTAS.

holy Purushottama. *poo-roo-SHOH-tah-mah* That wave which flows out of the OCEAN OF LOVE AND MERCY; the ECK.

Holy Spirit. ECK; DIVINE POWER; the sound of HU. *See also* DIVINE SPIRIT.

home of truth. The land of BHANWAR GUPHA and the Lord SOHANG, the plane of true miracles; the ETHERIC PLANE.

Honardi. *hoh-NAHR-dee* A spiritual community of ECK ADEPTS on the ATMA LOK, the SOUL PLANE.

Honu. *HOH-noo* A city on the CAUSAL PLANE, site of the SAKAPORI TEMPLE.

Hortar. *HOHR-tahr* The eleventh month of the ECK-VIDYA calendar, November, the days of wealth, the month of the pearl. SOUL begins to see liberation. *See also* JOURNEY OF SOUL.

House of Moksha. *MOHK-shah* The TEMPLE OF GOLDEN WISDOM in the PINDA LOK or physical world, in the city of RETZ, VENUS.

hrida chakra. *HREE-dah CHAH-krah* Also hridaya. Fourth of the body CHAKRAS; also called Dvadach-dal-Kanwal; near the cardia plexus; with twelve petals, it serves the circulation of the blood and breathing; the heart chakra. *See also* HEART CENTER.

hsin chai. *SIN CHIE* The FASTING mind; when thoughts are removed and one lives in the pure state.

hsu wu. *SOO WOO* State of emptiness and nonexistence; a deceptive state, for when all looks empty and nonexistent, the ECK MASTER appears in his RADIANT BODY.

HU. *HYOO* The secret name for God; the spirit CURRENT, the prime mover, and the first impulse that came from the Deity; also the first cause of motion, COLOR, and form. *See also* PRINCIPLE OF HU.

HU Chant. Also HU Song. A gathering of CHELAS to sing the ancient love song to God, the HU.

Huk. *HOOK* A word to be chanted for the AGAM LOK, the ninth plane; a state of SOUL in Its embodiment of truth, Hukikat.

Hukikat Purusha. *hoo-kee-KAHT poo-ROO-shah* The Lord of the HUKIKAT LOK, the plane of GOD-REALIZATION.

Hukikat Lok. *hoo-kee-KAHT LOHK* The plane of GOD-REALIZATION where SOUL learns GOD-KNOWLEDGE; the Eighth Plane.

HU, Law of. SPIRIT is the all-penetrating power which is the forming power of the universes of HU, the VOICE OF HU. *See also* LAWS OF THE PHYSICAL UNIVERSE.

H

Hum. *HYOOM* The word to be chanted on the ALAYA LOK, the seventh plane.

human consciousness. The negative, or earth, state of AWARENESS; the state of CONSCIOUSNESS used by the negative force as its CHANNEL.

humility. The opposite of VANITY, or AHANKARA; the absence of pride or VANITY; DINTA.

Huzur. *hoo-SHOOR* A title similar to Sir in addressing a man of God; not currently used in ECKANKAR.

Hyperboreans. *hie-pehr-bohr-EE-ahnz* The second ROOT RACE of mankind; this root race established the Melniboran empire in Africa under the VARKAS kings.

hypnotism. The worst of the psychic arts; a sleeplike condition psychically induced, which can be used to practice evil. Self-hypnotism cannot lead to SPIRITUAL UNFOLDMENT and is not a part of CONTEMPLATION. Practice of hypnotism can lead to a spiritual stalemate. In ECKANKAR hypnotism is not used, but is considered one of the THIRTY-TWO FACETS, or steps, on the path.

I

ida. *IE-dah* Ida is the CHANNEL at the right side of the spine, to the right of the central canal; PINGALA is the channel to the left, in the subtle body; the sushumna path of the occultist, through which the psychic force, or KUNDALINI, rises.

ignorance. Unawareness; not knowing; the root of all bondage in which man is bound.

illumination. *See* COSMIC CONSCIOUSNESS.

illusion. *See* MAYA.

imagination. A mental faculty that God has granted SOUL so that It may enter into the first door of the INNER WORLDS; a faculty which permits Soul to picture in thought. *See also* DIVINE FACULTY.

imaginative body. The ASTRAL BODY, or the EMOTIONAL BODY.

imaginative faculty. *See* DIVINE FACULTY.

imaginative technique. The process whereby the use of the IMAGINATION brings about SOUL TRAVEL; wherever thought goes, the spirit body must follow.

immortality. The state of being changeless and deathless, as opposed to mortality or being subject to change and DEATH.

impatience. One of the MANIFESTATIONS of ANGER, or KRODHA.

Inaccessible Plane. The AGAM LOK, the ninth plane; the word is HUK and the sound is the music of the woodwinds.

incarnations. The cycles of births and DEATHS in the lower worlds.

individual consciousness. The personal CONSCIOUSNESS or AWARENESS of self as a single being; the lowest of the CHANNELs through which the DIVINE SPIRIT manifests Itself. *See also* STATES OF CONSCIOUSNESS.

individuality. The divine, impersonal, and immortal self of man; the ECK, the LIGHT AND SOUND, is the symbol of individuality.

individual Soul. The manifested individual BEINGNESS of the ECK, or SPIRIT. *See also* ATMA.

Indra. *EEN-drah* The Hindu god of the ANGELS.

indri chakra. *EEN-dree CHAH-krah* Center of the sex organs, the generative center; SWADHISTANA center. The reproductive center in man, it lies near the sacral plexus; linga CHAKRA.

indriyas. *een-DREE-yahz* The sense organs: taste, smell, touch, hearing, and seeing.

indwelling power. The planted CONSCIOUSNESS of man in SPIRITUALITY; SPIRIT; the ECK.

I-ness. The ECK, SPIRIT, or SOUL within the individual.

infinite Spirit. Unlimited ESSENCE of love, WISDOM, and power, all three in one, undifferentiated, waiting to be differentiated by the individual CHANNELS. *See also* DIVINE SPIRIT; ECK.

initiate. One who has had the experience of being initiated by the LIVING ECK MASTER, who links him up with the ECK so that he will be lifted to higher spiritual levels.

initiation. The basic sacrament in ECK; the first step on the path of God via the ECK; the structure upon which the whole foundation of the spiritual works is built; the means by which the sacred forces within the individual are reactivated to increase and confer within SOUL the AWARENESS of the supernatural state of life.

inner altar. *See* COSMIC ALTAR OF GOD.

inner door. The opening through which man transcends the physical CONSCIOUSNESS and becomes aware of the spiritual self; closely guarded door at the top of the head where SOUL enters and leaves the body. *See also* TISRA TIL.

inner ear. The faculty within by which SOUL can hear the SOUND CURRENT, the ECK.

inner eye. *See* TISRA TIL.

inner initiation. Serves the function of raising the VIBRATIONS of the individual to those of the nearest higher plane. The inner initiation may come years before the outer initiation. The First Initiation is an inner initiation given in the DREAM STATE by the DREAM MASTER. Sometimes the chela is fully conscious and can remember everything about it; it prepares the CHELA for the linkup with the ECK SOUND CURRENT, the AUDIBLE LIFE STREAM. All initiations above the Eighth are inner initiations. *See also* INITIATION.

inner kingdom. CONSCIOUSNESS of the Divine.

Inner Master. LIGHT AND SOUND blended; the highest form of all love; the inner form of the LIVING ECK MASTER.

inner teachings. The teachings of ECKANKAR beyond the human state which enter into the depth of WISDOM—the best, highest, secret wisdom of all things; given by the ECK MASTERS mostly in the DREAM STATE or during SOUL TRAVEL at the TEMPLES OF GOLDEN WISDOM on the various inner planes.

inner vision. That AWARENESS of seeing which does not use the body's eyes, but sees with the inner eyes.

inner voice. The voice of the ECK, what some have called the still, small voice within.

69

inner world. The subjective relationship of man; the relationship with the invisible planes; the dimensions which are both within and without.

instant projection. The ability to move out of the PHYSICAL BODY, at will, into any of the higher STATES OF CONSCIOUSNESS; the SAGUNA SATI. *See also* ECK EXERCISES.

intellect. The capacity for rational thought; the study of various laws arising from the different relations of things to one another; not life in itself but a function of life; an effect and not the cause; does not create anything entirely new or constructive.

I

intelligence. One of the two aspects of the DIVINE POWER existing in the universe; the other is the LIFE-FORCE. Intelligence is that which is the source of CONSCIOUSNESS; intelligence and activity in the ECK POWER is the life-force in man.

intelligence ray. The fourth of the ten rays of the ECK which are sent out to the worlds below; the female, the passive potency, ray. *See also* ECK RAYS.

interdiluvian cycles. Great intervals of time during which the continents emerge from the seas.

intuition. A faculty of CONSCIOUSNESS connected with the NO-THING universe; the power of knowing, the power of obtaining knowing without the senses, without recourse to the inference of reasoning; an innate, instinctive knowledge.

invisible, the. The DIVINE POWER; the most powerful force; the greatest force in man; that which is not perceived by the physical senses.

Invisible Plane. The ALAKH LOK, or sixth plane; the word is SHANTI, and the sound is a heavy wind.

ionosphere. The ETHERIC PLANE; the land of BHANWAR GUPHA; the electrical mirror in the sky which reflects waves back to the earth.

iron. One of the nine metals which rule over the cycles of the sequence of the three in three in three, according to the ECK-VIDYA knowledge of cycles.

Iron Age. *See* KALI YUGA.

Ishtar. *EESH-tahr* The MAHANTA Consciousness as the vehicle for the SUGMAD as It was known to the Babylonians.

Ishwara. *eesh-WAH-rah* Another name for God; the MANIFESTATION of Brahman, Lord of the FOURTH PLANE, as manifested in three aspects: BRAHMA, the CREATOR; VISHNU, the preserver; and SHIVA, the destroyer.

Ismet Houdoni. *EES-meht hoo-DOH-nee* The LIVING ECK MASTER during the reign of James I of England, and who was his adviser; he is now on the CAUSAL PLANE working for the cause of ECK after translating at age 135.

Ism-i-Asm. *EESM-ee-AHSM* Another name for the ECK, the AUDIBLE LIFE CURRENT.

isness of the SUGMAD. The Supreme Being; the eternal Lord of all things; the everlasting Lord of all universes. *See also* SUGMAD TRINITY.

Isthul Sharir. *EES-thool shah-REER* The PHYSICAL BODY; man, the animal; it gets hurt, sick, and dies, to finally return to the soil.

IT, ITSELF. *See* SUGMAD.

J

jad. *JAHD* Materialism, as opposed to the ECK, which is the embodiment of all attributes of life.

jade, month of the. *See* GARVATA; JOURNEY OF SOUL.

Jagat Giri. *jah-GAHT GEE-ree* The title of the guardian of the SHARIYAT-KI-SUGMAD at the PARAM AKSHAR Temple on the ATMA LOK, or SOUL PLANE. This is currently TINDOR SAKI.

Jagat Ho. *jah-GAHT HOH* The LIVING ECK MASTER in China during the years 490–438 B.C. who is now on the ETHERIC PLANE as a CO-WORKER in the TEMPLE OF GOLDEN WISDOM there under LAI TSI.

Jaggannath. *JAH-gahn-nahth* Lord of the World; VISHNU; the physical universe; JOT NIRANJAN, the negative king of the physical world.

jagrat. *JAH-graht* The lowest quality of consciousness.

jal. *JAHL* Water and related subjects; one of the TATTWAS, the five PRIMARY STATES OF MATTER, the others being PRITHVI, VAYU, AKASH, and AGNI. *See* PRIMARY STATES OF MATTER.

Jalal ad-Din ar-Rumi. *jah-LAHL ahd-deen ar-ROO-mee* Thirteenth-century Persian sage and poet who had great spiritual knowledge and was a follower of ECK; he wrote the *Masnavi*. *See also* MASNAVI.

Jamdut. *jahm-DOOT* ANGEL OF DEATH, like the Yama Duta; an agent of the negative power, who meets all SOULS at the time of their DEATH unless they are with the LIVING ECK MASTER.

jananendriya. *jah-nah-NEHN-dree-yah* The five indriyas of knowledge, the cognitive senses of hearing, feeling, smelling, tasting, and seeing. *See also* INDRIYAS.

Janos Moneta. *JAH-nohs moh-NEH-tah* The LIVING ECK MASTER who lived near Stockholm, Sweden, and influenced Swedenborg during the eighteenth century; when he passed on, he went into the MENTAL PLANE to work.

jap. *JAHP* Mental repetition of a holy word.

J

Jaram Brahm. *jah-RAHM BRAHM* The one BEINGNESS of the poles of duality or seeming separateness; the poles of one being connected by two simultaneous CURRENTS of energy, the negative and positive, whose tension is the very condition for the MANIFES-TATION of what is within the being.

Jartz Chong. *JAHRTS CHOHNG* The TEMPLE OF GOLDEN WISDOM on the EIGHTH PLANE, or HUKIKAT LOK, also called Temple of the ALUK.

jasper, month of the. *See* JOURNEY OF SOUL; PARINAMA.

Jehovah. *jeh-HOH-vah* The MAHANTA Consciousness as the vehicle for the SUGMAD as It appeared to the old Judeans; also known as JOT NIRANJAN, a ruler of the ASTRAL PLANE.

Jeremiah. *jeh-reh-MIE-ah* A prophet of Israel, who was given the realization of the DIVINE POWER by the Lord and sent to do His work on earth.

Jesus. *JEE-zuhs* An ECK CHELA under ZADOK, the ECK MASTER in Judea, who gave him the basic fundamentals of ECK, and out of this knowledge came what is known today as Christianity.

jewels. Twelve stones which represent the months of the year in the ECK-VIDYA calendar: emerald, ASTIK; bloodstone, UTURAT; jade, GARVATA; opal, EBKIA; sapphire, RALOT; moonstone, SAHAK;

ruby, KAMITOC; diamond, MOKSHOVE; agate, DZYANI; jasper, PARI-NAMA; pearl, HORTAR; and onyx, NIYAMG. *See also* JOURNEY OF SOUL.

jewels of ECK. SOUL is always in ETERNITY, It is always in the present now, It is always in the heavenly state of the SUGMAD, and It exists because of God's love for It.

jhankar. *JAHN-kahr* Another name for the melodies of the lower worlds; a musical instrument.

Jiva. *JEE-vah* The Soul, or ATMA. *See also* SOUL.

Jivatma. *jee-VAHT-mah* Individual SOUL.

Jivan Mukti. *JEE-vahn MOOK-tee* Life everlasting; liberation, the salvation of SOUL during this lifetime; liberation of Soul from the rounds of births and DEATHS via the SOUND CURRENT; spiritual liberation during this lifetime; also called MOKSHA.

jnana. *JNAH-nah* The path of knowledge or learning; the same as GIANA, WISDOM.

Jnana Yoga. *JNAH-nah YOH-gah* A system of yoga which seeks SPIRITUAL LIBERATION through learning; works in the field of the MIND.

jot. *JAHT* Refers to the SAHASRA-DAL-KANWAL, or the lotus of a thousand petals; the CROWN CHAKRA.

Jot Niranjan. *JAHT nee-RAHN-jahn* The ruler of the physical universe; the being endowed with the negative power; the powerhouse of the physical universe, the PINDA world.

journey of Soul. The LIFE CYCLES of man, nations, and planets through which SOUL must pass in order to perfect Itself and return to Its heavenly home. *See* ASTIK; DZYANI; EBKIA; GARVATA; HORTAR; KAMITOC; MOKSHOVE; NIYAMG; PARINAMA; RALOT; SAHAK; UTURAT.

Joyti Basji. *joh-EE-tee BAHS-jee* The LIVING ECK MASTER in Mexico during the Mayan empire around the year 1055 B.C.

Ju Chiao. *JOO chee-AH-oh* The ECK MASTER in charge of the TEMPLE OF GOLDEN WISDOM on the SOUL PLANE, who was the LIVING ECK MASTER during the time of Hannibal, who had him killed.

Jupiter. The MAHANTA Consciousness as the vehicle for the SUGMAD as It appeared to the Romans.

J

K

ka. *KAH* Ancient Egyptian term for the ASTRAL BODY.

Kabir. *kah-BEER* The Hindu poet-mystic in the fifteenth and sixteenth centuries, a follower of ECK, who was the first to bring the mysteries of SOUL TRAVEL out into the open. For this he was hounded by both his Hindu and Muslim followers.

K

Kadath Inscriptions. *KAH-dahth* Old records which show the history of the LIVING ECK MASTERS throughout the universes; kept in the KATSUPARI MONASTERY in northern Tibet.

Kadmon. *KAD-mahn* The ECK MASTER in charge of the Temple of the ALUK or Temple of JARTZ CHONG on the HUKIKAT LOK, the eighth plane, where the sacred writings of the SHARIYAT-KI-SUGMAD are found; one of the highest of the ECK ADEPTS in the Order of the Vairagi, he was on earth during the infancy of man. As guardian of the Shariyat-Ki-Sugmad in Jartz Chong he is the ASANGA KAYA.

Kai-Kuas. *kie-KOO-ahs* The LIVING ECK MASTER during the time of the powerful, fierce, and ruthless VARKAS kings; he lived in secret and taught those who would listen until he was discovered by the Varkas and slain.

Kailash. *KIE-lahsh* One of three mountain peaks on the MENTAL PLANE, the other two are MER and SUMER. *See also* MER KAILASH.

Kaishvits. *KIE-shvits* The ninth ROOT RACE. A race from Mars who will conquer the earth and all the major planets after a major catastrophe spares only Mars. They will be in power for about five thousand years.

Kakusha. *kah-KOO-shah* One who has attained God.

Kal. *KAL* The negative; the negative power which is also used to denote the KAL NIRANJAN; that which is just.

kala. *kah-LAH* Time, which has many subdivisions; the word to be chanted for the ASTRAL PLANE.

Kalam. *kah-LAHM* The Muslim word for the SOUND CURRENT; a spiritual word.

Kalami-i-Lahi. *KAH-lahm-ee-ee-LAH-hee* One of the many names for the WORD of God, one of the Muslim words for the SOUND CURRENT.

Kali. *KAH-lee* The goddess of destruction; that which destroys all, yet replaces it with fertility of life; the sex goddess; goddess of time; wife of SHIVA; mother of all material CREATION; the six-armed goddess of blood and violence, the personification of the negative forces, and the FEMININE PRINCIPLE in the Universal Mind Force; in ECK, she is known as the Kalshar, the illusion of life, mother of KAL, the lady of Kala; in Christianity she is the virgin mother, the mother of saviors of the world, but not the ECK MASTERS who are born of the ECK POWER.

Kali Yuga. *KAH-lee YOO-gah* The Iron Age which is the dark era and last age of the MAHAYUGA (great yuga); it embraces one tenth, or 432,000, of the 4,320,000 years of the great yuga; one tenth of a day of God, or a KALPA; the last of the four ages of this day of God; the age in which the universe will be overwhelmed by darkness and decay and all will be destroyed in about 428,000 years by fire and ashes. *See also* MANVANTARA.

Kalma. *KAHL-mah* Another word for the SOUND CURRENT.

Kal Niranjan. *KAHL nee-RAHN-jahn* The negative MANIFESTATION of God through which the power flows to sustain the lower universes, whose VIBRATIONS are the coarser nature of matter; the CREATOR and lord of the physical worlds; god of space, the SPACE GOD; personification of negative.

kalpa. *KAHL-pah* A day of ETERNITY, or 4,320,000 man years; equal to a MANVANTARA, each divided into four YUGAS, or epochs:

K

Satya, Tretya, Dwapara, and Kali. *See also* DWAPARA YUGA; KALI YUGA; SATYA YUGA; TRETYA YUGA.

Kal power. The ten negative rays, beams, or forces which are the reverse of the ECK POWER. *See also* ECK RAYS.

Kal Purusha. *KAL poo-ROO-shah* The negative being, the predominating and presiding lord, the source of CREATIVE ENERGY for the negative in the negative or lower worlds; the DHARAM RAYA; BRAHM; KAL.

kama. *KAH-mah* Self-indulgence, which is the principle of sickness and evil in the KALI YUGA; LUST, or the degradation of sex; abnormal DESIRE which includes DRUGS, alcoholic drinks, tobacco, or foods eaten only for taste. *See also* FIVE PASSIONS OF THE MIND; SANTOSHA.

Kama Rupa. *KAH-mah ROO-pah* The ASTRAL BODY, or form, in which passion resides, or is expressed; the Astral form that exists after DEATH of the PHYSICAL BODY; the ghost form, or sometimes a vampire who returns to those who long for them out of loneliness.

kamit. *KAH-mit* The LAW OF SILENCE, which means being silent about the secret teachings, personal affairs with ECK, and the personal word given in the INITIATIONS.

Kamitoc. *KAH-mee-tahk* The seventh month of the ECK-VIDYA calendar, July, called the days of freedom, the month of the ruby. In this JOURNEY OF SOUL, freedom comes through knowledge.

Kangra Sambha. *KAHN-grah SAHM-bah* The passing of SOUL from the PHYSICAL BODY at the DEATH of the temple of clay; the supraspiritual experience of Soul, or journey from the Physical to the ASTRAL PLANE.

kani. *KAH-nee* The EGO, or opposite of HUMILITY.

kanth chakra. *KAHNTH CHAH-krah* The microcosmic center in the body, located near the cervical plexus which has to do with respiration; SHAT-DAS-DAL-KANWAL, the lotus of sixteen petals, the throat center. *See also* CHAKRA(S); MICROCOSMIC CENTERS; VISHUDHA CHAKRA.

Kanwal. *KAHN-wahl* The lotus shape of the CHAKRAS, or MICROCOS-MIC CENTERS, in the PHYSICAL BODY.

Karan mind. *KAH-rahn* The true, or Causal, MIND which works in the BRAHMANDA worlds; the NIJ MIND, inner mind; the mind of the CAUSAL PLANE.

Karan Sarup. *KAH-rahn sah-ROOP* Also called KARAN SHARIR, or Karma Sarup; the seed body; the sheath wherein is planted the cause of karma; the body SOUL uses on the CAUSAL PLANE.

Karan Sharir. *KAH-rahn shah-REER* The CAUSAL, or seed body, which contains all that has ever or is ever to take place in an individual's life. *See also* KARAN SARUP.

karma bandhan. *KAR-mah bahn-DAHN* The bonds of karma, or actions; being bound to the chains of action.

karma kanda. *KAR-mah KAHN-dah* The path of actions; the way of salvation by right actions.

Karma, Law of. *KAR-mah* The Law of CAUSE AND EFFECT, action and reaction, justice, retribution, and reward, which applies to the lower or PSYCHIC WORLDS: the PHYSICAL, ASTRAL, CAUSAL, MENTAL, and ETHERIC PLANES; the Law of Universal Compensation which is under the Law of Vibration; inflow and outflow; a matter of VIBRATIONS; one of the twelve laws by which the universes are sustained. *See also* KRIYAMAN KARMA; PRAABDH KARMA.

Karma, Lord of. *See* DHARAM RAYA.

Karma Marg. *KAR-mah MAHRG* The way of karma as a path to God; the approach to God through selflessness and harmonious deeds.

Karma Yoga. *KAHR-mah YOH-gah* The yoga of action; the ideal of duty well done and the VAIRAG, the spirit of unattachment.

karmendriya. *kahr-MEHN-dree-yah*   The power of action in all physical activities.

karmic pattern. *KAHR-mik*   The particular way in which an individual acts and reacts throughout the experiences of many lives.

karuna. *kah-ROO-nah*   Active COMPASSION.

Kassapa. *kah-SAH-pah*   The LIVING ECK MASTER before the destruction of ATLANTIS.

Kata Daki. *KAH-tah DAH-kee*   An ECK MASTER in the Ancient Order of the Vairagi, who is a woman.

Katsupari Monastery. *kaht-soo-PAH-ree*   An ECK monastery and TEMPLE OF GOLDEN WISDOM in the BUIKA MAGNA mountain range of northern Tibet under the guardianship of the ECK Master, FUBBI QUANTZ.

Kaya Kalp. *KAH-yah KAHLP*   A system of renewing the health and youth of the PHYSICAL BODY; also called AYUR VEDHA; means lifetime.

Kazi Dawtz. *KAH-zee DAHTS*   The TEMPLE OF GOLDEN WISDOM on the AGAM LOK, the ninth plane, or the fifth of the God Worlds; also called the Temple of AKASH.

Ketu Jaraul. *KEH-too ja-RAHL*   A LIVING ECK MASTER who was the secret adviser for Charlemagne, teaching him the secrets of ECK and helping with his spiritual problems.

kevala. *keh-VAH-lah*   Means alone.

Kevalshar. *KEHV-ahl-shahr*   The INITIATE of the Eleventh Circle; the entrance into the SUGMAD world.

key to spiritual worlds.   The VAIRAG state which is DETACHMENT from worldly DESIRES and a mental love of the world; the state of successful detachment from worldly things; nonattachment, which does not reject all material things and live in a state of nonbeing, but is not attached to them.

K

Khara Khota. *KAH-rah KOH-tah* The capital city of the empire of UIGHUR in central Asia in the Gobi Desert during the time of the fifth ROOT RACE, the ARYANS.

Khashathra-Vairya. *KAH-shah-thrah-VIER-yah* One of the six ways the supreme SUGMAD has to make ITSELF known to man; one of six rays of light from the Divine known as the AMESHA SPENTAS; the all-creative, all-sustaining power.

Kimtaved. *keem-TAH-vehd* Located in South America, it is one of the seven SPIRITUAL CITIES on earth to help this world.

kingdom of ECK. The true KINGDOM OF GOD. The totality of all there is, all planes; all that is and all that is not.

Kingdom of God. The CONSCIOUSNESS of God within SOUL; heaven; the HEAVENLY KINGDOM; the heaven of heavens; paradise; Eden; the holy city; God's throne; the city celestial; the abode of the Blessed.

kingdom of heaven. That realm of SPIRIT where God, the SUGMAD, has established ITS fountainhead in the universe of universes; the true home of SOUL.

kingdom of the SUGMAD. The ultimate, imperishable, highest of all the spiritual regions; the ANAMI, the nameless region; the beginning and ending of all worlds; the love and power of the SUGMAD, the first principle, which vibrates throughout the worlds.

King of the Dead. YAMA, the judge who presides at the court where all uninitiated SOULS must go to receive judgment for their earthly actions. *See also* DHARAM RAYA.

kinslo nibbana. *KEEN-sloh nee-BAHN-ah* Death of moral defilements. *See also* NIBBUTA.

Kitai. *KEE-tie* The enlightened one; the second stage of INITIATION on the path of ECK. *See also* ARAHATA.

Kita Sorgi. *KEE-tah SOR-gee* An ECK MASTER during the time of Alexander the Great, who went with him to visit the Oracle of Ammon in Egypt.

Klemp, Harold. The present MAHANTA, the LIVING ECK MASTER who received the ROD OF ECK POWER at midnight of October 22, 1981, from Darwin Gross under the direction of REBAZAR TARZS, the Torchbearer of ECKANKAR. The spiritual name of SRI Harold Klemp is WAH Z.

Koji Chanda. *KOH-jee CHAHN-dah* The title of the guardian of the SHARIYAT-KI-SUGMAD on the PAR BRAHM LOK, the Fourth, or MENTAL, PLANE, at the NAMAYATAN TEMPLE OF GOLDEN WISDOM in the city of MER KAILASH. This is currently TOWART MANAGI.

Krishna. *KREESH-nah* The MAHANTA Consciousness as the vehicle for the SUGMAD as It was known to the Hindus.

Krita Yuga. *See* SATYA YUGA.

kriyaman karma. *KREE-yah-mahn KAR-mah* Karma which is made hour to hour and day to day; daily karma; new karma created by actions during this life. *See also* KARMA, LAW OF.

Kriya Yoga. *See* KARMA YOGA.

krodha. *KROH-dah* ANGER, one of the five destructive actions of the MIND; tantrums, fury, mental carcinoma, slander, evil gossip, backbiting, profanity, faultfinding, jealousy, malice, impatience, resentment, mockery, destructive criticism, and ill will. *See also* KSHAMA.

Kros, Records of the. *KROHS* The ancient transcripts of the past history of this earth planet and what will become of it; history and prophecy kept in the KATSUPARI MONASTERY in the BUIKA MAGNA mountain range.

kshama. *KSHAH-mah* Forgiveness and tolerance; the remedy for KRODHA, ANGER.

Kumba Mehla. *KOOM-bah MEH-lah* A religious fair held every twelve years in India, as a reflection of the TRIBENI at the top of the CAUSAL PLANE where three streams meet.

kundalini. *koon-dah-LEE-nee* That great force which lies in the reproductive center of man, near the coccyx, below the sacral plexus; the sex force; the SWADHISTANA CHAKRA.

Kundun. *KOON-DOON* The presence of the LIVING ECK MASTER.

Kuritee. *koo-REE-tee* The sixth twelve-year cycle in the DUODE-NARY CYCLE of man's spiritual journey called the Years of the Strange Storms. *See* CYCLES OF TWELVE.

Kurnai. *KEHR-nie* The INITIATE of the Third Circle. *See also* AHRAT.

kykeôn. *KIE-keh-ohn* A beverage like the ambrosia or nectar used at the Eleusinian initiation.

L

lac. *LAHK* The equivalent of one hundred thousand years; a section of time in the physical universe.

lakh(s). *See* LAC.

Lai Tsi. *LIE TSEE* The Chinese ECK MASTER who is the guardian of the SHARIYAT-KI-SUGMAD on the SAGUNA LOK, the ETHERIC PLANE, at the TEMPLE OF GOLDEN WISDOM in the city of ARHIRIT.

Lamakan. *LAH-mah-kahn* The region of the endless, the original or the eternal; from it all other regions are created or manifested; the beyond all, which cannot even be termed as a plane or a region. *See also* AKAHA.

Lamotta. *lah-MOT-tah* The LIVING ECK MASTER who accepted the ROD OF ECK POWER in the year 1000 B.C. and was slain by a band of Assyrians, as he worked to spread the word of ECK during the time of David the King; he is now assisting RAMI NURI at the TEMPLE OF GOLDEN WISDOM on VENUS.

lam-rim. *LAHM-REEM* Stages on the ECK path.

Lao-tzu. *low-TSOO* Sixth-century B.C. Chinese philosopher who wrote the *Tao Te Ching*.

Law of Attitudes. *See* ATTITUDES, LAW OF.

Law of Balance. *See* BALANCE, LAW OF; POLARITY, LAW OF.

Law of Cause and Effect. *See* KARMA, LAW OF.

Law of Consciousness. *See* CONSCIOUSNESS, LAW OF.

Law of Creativity. *See* CREATIVITY, LAW OF.

Law of Dharma. *See* DHARMA.

Law of Facsimiles. *See* FACSIMILES, LAW OF.

Law of God. *See* GOD, LAW OF.

Law of Grace. *See* GRACE, LAW OF.

Law of Harmonics. *See* VIBRATIONS, LAW OF.

Law of HU. *See* HU LAW OF; LAWS OF THE PHYSICAL UNIVERSE.

Law of Karma. *See* KARMA, LAW OF.

Law of Life. *See* DHARMA.

Law of Love. *See* LOVE, LAW OF.

Law of Manu. *See* MANU, LAW OF.

Law of Mksha. *See* MKSHA; MKSHA, LAW OF.

Law of Opposites. *See* POLARITY, LAW OF.

Law of Polarity. *See* POLARITY, LAW OF.

Law of Retribution. *See* KARMA, LAW OF.

Law of Reversed Effort. *See* REVERSED EFFORT, LAW OF.

Law of Silence. *See* KAMIT.

Law of Soul. *See* SOUL, LAW OF.

Law of Spirit. *See* SPIRIT, LAW OF.

Law of Spiritual Growth. *See* SPIRITUAL GROWTH, LAW OF.

Law of Unity. *See* UNITY, LAW OF.

Law of Vibrations. *See* KARMA, LAW OF; LAWS OF THE PHYSICAL UNIVERSE; VIBRATIONS, LAW OF.

Law, Righteous. *See* DANDA.

laws of nature. The laws of the negative power; the LAWS OF THE PHYSICAL UNIVERSE; the natural laws.

laws of the physical universe. The BOOK OF LAWS; seven fundamental laws that govern the physical universe through SPIRIT: LAW OF ATTITUDES, LAW OF FACSIMILES, LAW OF HU, LAW OF POLARITY, LAW OF SOUL, LAW OF UNITY, and LAW OF VIBRATIONS.

Law, Universal. *See* POLARITY, LAW OF.

Laya Center. *LAH-yah* That mystical point of no return when SOUL crosses from one plane into another and is prepared to stay and never to return to the lower one.

Laya Yoga. *LAH-yah YOH-gah* Consists of the absorption of the MIND in the ASTRAL LIGHT, through the practice of MUDRA exercises.

Lemuria. *leh-MOOR-ee-ah* The continent of MU, which had the greatest civilization known to the world; the Empire of the Sun; destroyed by earthquakes and sunk into the Pacific Ocean.

Lemurians. *leh-MOOR-ee-ahnz* The third ROOT RACE, highly civilized and spiritual, who lived on the continent of MU, LEMURIA.

Lenurig. *leh-NOO-reeg* The seventh twelve-year cycle in the DUODENARY CYCLE called the Years of the Wandering Seas, according to the ECK-VIDYA DOCTRINE OF CYCLES. *See also* CYCLES OF TWELVE.

Lhokhor. *LOH-kohr* The twelve-year cycle of the spiritual growth of man. *See also* CYCLES OF TWELVE; RABJUNG.

liberation, spiritual. *See* JIVAN MUKTI.

life. BEING; the experience of STATES OF CONSCIOUSNESS; life is SPIRIT, and Spirit is static; the Sound; the ECK.

life current. Love is the profound CURRENT of life.

life cycles. *See* JOURNEY OF SOUL.

Life Force. That which is conscious of Itself; the SUGMAD, God; DIVINE POWER, whose other aspect is INTELLIGENCE.

life principle. *See* PRINCIPLE OF LIFE.

Life Stream. *See* DIVINE POWER.

Light. The reflection of the spiritual atoms moving in space, as the ECK, the MANIFESTATION of the SUGMAD in the lower worlds, flows from the SUGMAD into them and returns.

Light and Sound. The ECK as the MANIFESTATION in the lower worlds of the absolute supreme Deity, the SUGMAD.

Light body. The Nuri Sarup; the SUKHSHAM SHARIR; the body sheath of SOUL for the ASTRAL PLANE.

Light Giver. The LIVING ECK MASTER; the VI-GURU; the GODMAN.

Lightning Worlds. Subplanes which lie between the PHYSICAL PLANE and the true ASTRAL PLANE. *See also* MOON WORLDS; SUN WORLDS.

lila. *LEE-lah* Singing and dancing made up of sound, silence, motion, and rest which SOUL does as a result of GOD-REALIZATION; the play of Soul.

linga chakra. *See* INDRI CHAKRA.

lingam. *LEEN-gahm* Passion and its bonds.

Linga Sharir. *LEEN-gah shah-REER* The ASTRAL BODY; the SUBTLE BODY, Karma Rupa, which expresses passion; similar to the PHYSICAL BODY in appearance.

Living ECK Master. The VI-GURU, the GODMAN; the ECK personified, the true and competent Master who works for the freedom of enslaved SOULS, leading them beyond and out of the LOWER

PLANES of existence into SELF-REALIZATION; the living embodiment
of all that is religious, the spirit of life lying dormant in others;
the AWAKENED SOUL, transcending time and space and CAUSATION,
holding the past, present, and future in the palm of his hand.
Appointed to his high position, he is expected to defend the God
power, the works of ECK, and the CHELAS who have put their
interest and trust in the ECK. He is not allowed to retire from
his field of action in this life until another is ready and trained
to replace him; when his position is attacked by revolt or
dissatisfaction among the followers of ECK, he will be defended
from the inner planes by means of the ECK; those who attack
the Master will receive the swiftest retribution, which does not
come from the Master himself, but from the ECK. All Living
ECK Masters have descended from the first ECK MASTER, GAKKO,
who came into this world about six million years ago; some have
been married, others are single; they have all served the ECK
faithfully, giving their lives to It. *See also* MAHANTA.

living Quintan. *See* QUINBODIES.

living truth. Every SOUL is still living and has been in existence
since the beginning of this universe; no Soul has ever been
destroyed.

lobha. *LOHB-hah*   GREED; one of the FIVE PASSIONS OF THE MIND; mi-
serliness, lying, hypocrisy, perjury, misrepresentation, robbery,
bribery, and trickery of all sorts. *See also* DISCRIMINATION; FIVE
PASSIONS OF THE MIND; VIVEKA.

Logos. *LOH-gohs*   The WORD of God, NAM; inner reality; the DIVINE
SPIRIT which gives life to all.

lok. *LOHK*   The word for plane. *See also* PLANES.

longevity. Living in a human body far beyond what is considered
to be the normal life span, such as is the case of many ECK
ADEPTS of the Order of the Vairagi, some of whom are hundreds
of years old.

Lords of Karma. *KAR-mah*   The group of entities under the
DHARAM RAYA, the distributor of KARMA, who are responsible for
the distribution of the ADI-KARMA, or primal karma, to SOULS first

entering this world, and for adding and subtracting karma from the records of any Soul in the lower worlds.

Lotus of the Fiery Light. CROWN CHAKRA; set of ten laws the seeker of God must understand before going into the ANAMI LOK; the golden LIGHT which is never manifested; the formless and silent.

lotus, thousand-petaled. *See* CROWN CHAKRA.

love. Feeling that imparts vitality to THOUGHT; feeling is DESIRE, and desire is love; the adhesive force that holds everything together; the doctrine of universal unity, the oneness of the SUGMAD; a dichotomy whose opposite is hate in the lower worlds; the ECK; the universal law of all laws; the DIVINE ESSENCE which unites all reality and brings together all SOULS; the bond which holds the worlds together.

Love, Law of. The principle which gives THOUGHT the dynamic power to correlate with its object, and, therefore, to master every adverse human experience; feeling that imparts vitality to thought; feeling is DESIRE, and desire is love.

lower mind. *See* MIND.

lower planes. The PHYSICAL, ASTRAL, CAUSAL, MENTAL, and ETHERIC, PLANES which are the schools of experience for SOUL.

lower worlds. The PLANES below the SOUL PLANE; the worlds of energy, matter, time, and space. *See also* LOWER PLANES.

lunar body. The counterpart of the PHYSICAL BODY which is part of the AURA; if it is withdrawn from the physical body, DEATH results; cannot be seen with the physical eyes.

lust. KAMA, one of the FIVE PASSIONS OF THE MIND.

M

macrocosm. The God Worlds, including all universes; the universal world; that which is reflected in the MICROCOSM, man.

Madhava. *mah-DAH-vah* A title meaning KRISHNA, the Godlike CONSCIOUSNESS.

Magi. *MAY-jie* A mystical order of the Zoroastrian religion, one of the ancient groups which secretly studied ECK and practiced It six hundred years before Christ.

magic. The producing of phenomena or controlling of events by the use of charms or rituals; part of the Universal MIND Power, the KAL force, it brings upon the practitioner the effect, or karma.

Maha. *MAH-hah* Great one.

Maha Kal. *MAH-hah KAL* The God who rules the universes of matter; the supreme deity of all the known regions of the physical universe; PAR BRAHM; KAL NIRANJAN, who rules over negative reality and affects all below.

Maha Kal Lok. *MAH-hah KAL LOHK* The MIND world; the MENTAL PLANE; the fourth plane.

maha kalpa. *MAH-hah KAL-pah* Seven cosmic days of the SUGMAD; equal to seven KALPAS. *See also* MAHAYUGA, MANVANTARA; PRALAYA.

Mahamai. *MAH-hah-mie* Great mother; the KALI; the sex goddess.

maha manvantara. *MAH-hah mahn-vahn-TAH-rah* See MAHA KALPA, MAHAYUGA; MANVANTARA.

Maha Nada. *MAH-hah NAH-dah* The great music of the ECK LIFE CURRENT.

Mahanta. *mah-HAHN-tah* The INITIATE of the Fourteenth Circle; the Mahanta, the LIVING ECK MASTER; the full force of the ROD OF ECK POWER and the Mantle of the Mahanta are embodied directly in him; all those who come to him in the present age have been with him since their advent into the world; the body of the Mahanta is the ECK, which is the ESSENCE of God flowing out from the OCEAN OF LOVE AND MERCY, sustaining all life and tying together all life-forms; the VI-GURU, the LIGHT GIVER; a state of GOD CONSCIOUSNESS which is beyond the titles given in religions which designate states of CONSCIOUSNESS; the highest of all STATES OF CONSCIOUSNESS. This special incarnation of the SUGMAD makes an appearance but once every five to a thousand or more years, depending upon the part he is to play in a major upliftment of consciousness on every plane.

M

Mahanta Maharai. *mah-HAHN-tah MAH-hah-rie* The INITIATE of the THIRTEENTH CIRCLE in the ECK works; the LIVING ECK MASTER who is aware of his relationship to the MAHANTA Consciousness.

Maharaj. *mah-hah-RAHJ* The Brotherhood of ECK MASTERS, subordinate to the MAHANTA, the LIVING ECK MASTER who holds the ROD OF ECK POWER.

Maharaji. *mah-hah-RAH-jee* The INITIATE of the TWELFTH CIRCLE in ECKANKAR, the LIVING ECK MASTER but not the MAHANTA. *See also* MAHANTA MAHARAI.

maha rishi. *MAH-hah REE-shee* Superior to those who have gained the singular title of RISHI, but not a SPIRITUAL MASTER; maha means great one.

Maha Sunna. *MAH-hah SOON-nah* The top of the third plane, or CAUSAL WORLD, where the center of the vast area is pitch darkness; the empty realm wherein all disturbance and agitation of SOUL is calmed.

mahat. *MAH-haht* THOUGHT; the first changed form of the nature elements; matter, space, time, and twenty-two other parts of the Universal MIND force.

Mahatma. *mah-HAHT-mah* Great SOUL; *maha* means "great," and *ATMA* means "Soul."

Mahavakyis. *mah-hah-VAHK-yeez* The silent travelers; the Silent Ones; agents of the SUGMAD who are responsible only to IT; they are in command of the great SOUND CURRENT, and give aid and comfort to the SUGMAD in ITS eternal home, as well as being in charge of the mechanical phases of the lower universes.

Mahaya Guru. *mah-HAH-yah GOO-roo* The title of the guardian of the holy book, the SHARIYAT-KI-SUGMAD, on the AGAM LOK, the ninth plane, at the KAZI DAWTZ TEMPLE OF GOLDEN WISDOM; this is currently AGNOTTI.

mahayuga. *mah-hah-YOO-gah* The cycle for COSMIC HISTORY of a day of the SUGMAD, or 4,320,000 years, which consists of four ages, or YUGAS. *See also* MANVANTARA.

M

Mahdis. *MAH-dees* The INITIATE of the FIFTH CIRCLE (SOUL PLANE); often used as a generic term for all High Initiates in ECK; the ECK and Its message is distributed through the MAHANTA, the LIVING ECK MASTER to each of the Mahdis for every plane in the lower worlds; the key to the survival of ECKANKAR in this world is the Mahanta, the Living ECK Master working with the Mahdis, the initiates of the Fifth Circle, who are his chief CHANNELS of the ECK POWER; the Mahdis are able to work only in this world and in the first five PLANES as distributors of the ECK power. *See also* FIFTH INITIATION.

Malati. *mah-LAH-tee* The first ECK MASTER of record among the POLARIANS who was sent by the SUGMAD to give man his first spiritual knowledge of God.

man. The first of the individuated forms of CREATION inhabited by that spark of God, SOUL, which has the ability to become aware of Itself as divine INTELLIGENCE and can become God-Realized; the MICROCOSM which reflects the MACROCOSM; body and Soul through which the ECK becomes individuated in the lower worlds.

Mana. *MAH-nah* Word for the CAUSAL PLANE. A CHANT.

Manas. *MAH-nahs* One of the four ANTISHKARANS (modes of action of the MIND); the mind stuff (Universal MIND Power), which has the power to receive feeling, taste, smell, and hearing. Its chief attribute is taste.

mandala. *mahn-DAH-lah* Hindu term for a circle; a kind of emblem, in the form of a ritual geometric diagram; a means toward CONTEMPLATION and concentration.

manifestation. That which is apparent to the physical senses; the LIVING ECK MASTER is the manifestation of God in the physical flesh; at the center of all manifestation there is only one God.

manipurak chakra. *mahn-ee-POO-rahk CHAH-krah* The third psychic center of the lower universe in the PHYSICAL BODY near the navel, the eight-petaled lotus. In ECKANKAR known as the NABHI CHAKRA, or ASHTA-DAL-KANWAL.

Manmukh. *MAHN-mook* One of the two groups of all mankind; those who follow their own MINDS, obeying the mind's every whim, a slave to it and its passions. *See also* GURUMUKH.

Mansarover. *MAHN-sah-roh-vehr* In the world of DASWAN DWAR, a stream of the sweet nectar of the heavenly gods which flows out of a lake of the same name; the river of IMMORTALITY.

mantra. *MAHN-trah* The word which, when chanted, is the ECK POWER; an instrument for linking up with the ECK; the word of action, a deed immediately calling forth reality; not merely a sound but an action of the ECK in motion.

mantram(s). *See* MANTRA.

Mantra Yoga. *MAHN-trah YOH-gah* A system of yoga aiming at acquiring psychic powers in the astral regions by constant repetition of certain formulas which are supposed to set up particular VIBRATIONS when repeated with the MIND fixed upon certain centers.

Manu, Law of. Hindu code of laws which established a caste system; part of the evolution of the social CONSCIENCE.

Manu Samhita. *MAH-noo sahm-HEE-tah* The ECKANKAR code of ethics.

Manushi. *mah-NOO-shee* Human embodiment; the LIVING ECK MASTER in the flesh; the MAHANTA who can be seen.

manvantara. *mahn-vahn-TAH-rah* The cycle of COSMIC HISTORY, or a day of the SUGMAD, which embraces the SATYA YUGA, the Golden Age, 1,728,000 years or four tenths of the cycle; the TRETYA YUGA, the Silver Age, 1,296,000 years or three tenths of the cycle; the DWAPARA YUGA, the Copper Age, 864,000 years or two tenths of the cycle; and the KALI YUGA, the Iron, or Dark, Age, 432,000 years or one tenth of the cycle. *See also* MAHAYUGA.

mara. *MAH-rah* The Buddhist word for the world of psychic reality; in Christianity, Satan, or the DEVIL; in the works of ECK, the KAL NIRANJAN, the king of the lower worlds.

mardang. *mar-DAHNG* A type of long drum.

Marfat. *MAHR-faht* The stage of development of man which represents the nearness to and communion with the ECK SPIRIT; the SELF-REALIZATION level.

marg. *MAHRG* A path to God. *See* ARAHATA MARG; BHAKTI MARG; ECK MARG; GIANI MARG; KARMA MARG; PRAPATTI MARG; VAHANA MARG.

Mariolatry. In Christian thought, the worship of the Virgin Mary.

masculine principle. The male is positive, active, and progressive; it devises but it never creates; it discovers and works out the principles of God; it plans, correlates, and gives birth to social order, systems of religious and philosophical thoughts, and ideas.

Masnavi. *mahs-NAH-vee* A book of poems or couplets written by JALAL AD-DIN AR-RUMI, the Persian poet and mystic, to express the glory and love of God.

Masters. *See* ECK MASTERS.

mat. *MAHT* Creed or doctrine.

Matax Roraka. *MAH-taks roh-RAH-kah* Appointed by Vajra Manjushri around 700 B.C. as the Living ECK Master to succeed him when he was executed by King Hakhamanish I of Persia.

material universe. The world of energy, matter, space, and time; the everchanging; that of momentary existence; illusion, MAYA; unreality.

Mauj. *mah-OOJ* Will or pleasure of the Sat Guru, or the supreme one.

Maulani. *mah-oo-LAH-nee* The INITIATE of the NINTH CIRCLE in ECKANKAR; a Co-WORKER with the SUGMAD; candidate for possible ECK Mastership.

mauna. *mah-OO-nah* Communication by mental telepathy.

M

maya. *MAH-yah* The way man looks at reality; the KAL NIRANJAN, or Kal-maya; the illusion of reality; that which has been torn from reality and is limited in time and space; part of the CREATIVE PRINCIPLE within the limitations of the HUMAN CONSCIOUSNESS; impermanence.

McWilliams Law. All particles are moving in space according to their own pattern but never crashing or interfering with one another.

Mearp region. *meh-AHRP* Where the SOUL records of the MAHDIS are kept, within the ATMA PLANE.

mechanical manifestations. Lying, imagination, the expression of negative emotions, and unnecessary talking.

meditation. The passive way, or technique, of trying to reach the GODHEAD; making use of the FEMININE PRINCIPLE in order to accomplish that which is neither feminine nor masculine; a passive state in which the practitioner tries to draw GOD-REALIZATION into himself to attain oneness with God.

Melnibora. *mehl-NEE-boh-rah* The mighty empire of the Hyper-boreans, the second root race; ruled by the fierce Varkas kings for a hundred centuries.

Mental body. The body for the Mental Plane; the transformer for thought between the mind and the Astral body.

Mental Plane. The fourth of the planes of the lower worlds; source of philosophy, ethics, moral teachings, and aesthetics; seat of the Universal Mind Power; the sound here is running water.

Mental Sharir. *See* Mental body.

Mer. *MEHR* One of three mountain peaks on the Mental Plane; the other two are Sumer and Kailash.

Mer Kailash. *MEHR KIE-lahsh* The city on the Mental Plane where the Shariyat-Ki-Sugmad is kept in the Temple of Golden Wisdom; sometimes called Mersumer Kailash after the three mountain peaks of Brahm Lok: Mer, Sumer, and Kailash.

Mersumer Kailash. *See* Mer Kailash.

Mesi Gokaritz. *MEH-see goh-KAHR-eets* The Living ECK Master in the early days of Greece who is the Tsong Sikhsa, the guardian of the Shariyat-Ki-Sugmad at the Anakamudi Temple on the Alaya Lok, the seventh plane.

message of ECK. The Living ECK Master gives the message of ECK, which is the Light and Sound of the SUGMAD; in silence one practices the Spiritual Exercises of ECK, as given by the Master, and finds the heavenly world; no one can find it any other way.

metta. *MEHT-tah* Goodwill, love.

microcosm. The small universe; man is the microcosm of the vast macrocosm which comprises all creation; the body of each indi-vidual is the microcosm in which the macrocosm dwells.

microcosmic centers. The smaller microcosms which are located in the body of man and have a definite relation to some portion of the outlying universe; CHAKRAS, or universes; the clusters of universes which make up the body of man, the smaller universe. *See also* CHAKRA(S).

middle path. The neuter, or middle, way; neither positive nor negative; neither masculine (forcing) nor feminine (passive); balance between the negative and the positive; the balanced, well-adjusted outlook of the middle way; neither being for nor against.

Milarepa. *mi-lah-REH-pah* An eleventh-century Tibetan saint and poet who was an ECK MASTER.

mind. Mind is matter, but it stands next to SOUL in the ESSENCE of its own being; its chief function is only to serve as an instrument for SPIRIT to make all Its contact with the material worlds; the CHANNEL through which the negative force, or KAL NIRANJAN, controls and keeps SOUL in the lower worlds through the FIVE PASSIONS OF THE MIND. There is only one mind acting on different PLANES: PINDA, or lower-world, mind manifesting in the common affairs of the world; SUKHSHAM MIND, the mind of the ASTRAL PLANE, the emotions; and the KARAN, the Nij, the inner, the causal mind, the memories.

Mind body. *See* MIND; NIJ MANAS.

mind, faculties of. The four primary attributes, faculties, or qualities of mind called ANTISHKARANS. *See also* AHANKAR; BUDDHI; CHITTA; MANAS.

mind travel. The ability to move about in the other worlds in the thought body; one of the higher steps in spiritual development.

mineral state. The mineral kingdom. The state in which CONSCIOUSNESS (SOUL) sleeps imprisoned in the rocklike substance of minerals.

Mksha. *MUHK-shah* An ancient ECK sage who appeared on earth some 35,000 years ago to teach the people of the Indus Valley the fundamental laws which govern the physical universe. *See also* LAWS OF THE PHYSICAL UNIVERSE.

Mksha, Law of. *MUHK-shah* Life is only SPIRIT, and being Spirit, it has nothing; it has only INTELLIGENCE with the peculiar ability to perceive, penetrate, and survive, and have CAUSATION, specialization, CREATIVENESS, beauty, love, and ethics.

moha. *MOH-hah* Delusive ATTACHMENT, infatuation, procrastination, worries, anxieties, and business complications; the opposite of DETACHMENT; one of the five destructive passions of the mind. *See also* FIVE PASSIONS OF THE MIND; VAIRAG.

Moksha. *MOHK-shah* Release from the WHEEL OF AWAGAWAN, birth, DEATH, and rebirth in the lower worlds; liberation from this wheel through the MAHANTA.

Moksha, House of. *MOHK-shah* The TEMPLE OF GOLDEN WISDOM in the city of RETZ on the planet VENUS where RAMI NURI is in charge of the SHARIYAT-KI-SUGMAD.

Mokshove. *mohk-SHOHV* The eighth month of the ECK-VIDYA calendar, August, called the days of light, the month of the diamond; the translation of spiritual knowledge into great truths by SOUL. *See also* JOURNEY OF SOUL.

molds. The thoughts, attitudes, and images of the MIND which are filled by SPIRIT and manifest in life; thus every thought, image, or attitude will manifest sooner or later as an event in life.

mondo. *MOHN-doh* Questions and answers between the Master and CHELA; usually pithy.

moonstone, month of the. *See* JOURNEY OF SOUL; SAHAK.

Moon Worlds. Subplanes which lie between the PHYSICAL PLANE and the true ASTRAL PLANE. *See also* LIGHTNING WORLDS; SUN WORLDS.

Moraji Desal. *moh-RAH-jee deh-SAHL* The LIVING ECK MASTER who followed GOPAL DAS and helped to write the Hammurabic Code of Laws.

Mountain of Light. The mountain of SAHASRA-DAL-KANWAL; the powerhouse of the Astral and the Physical, or PINDA, universe;

99

a huge dynamo out of which flows all the power that creates and sustains all the CREATIONS below it.

Mu. *MOO* The no-mind state; negative; below the usual state of negativism. Also another name for LEMURIA, a continent in the Pacific destroyed by earthquakes; a land in the misty past of time where SOUL TRAVEL was taught by ECK MASTERS.

mudra. *MOO-drah* Exercises used in LAYA YOGA to achieve the absorption of the MIND into the ASTRAL LIGHT.

Mukam Taq. *MOO-kahm TAHK* The FAR COUNTRY, or another name for SAT DESHA, true country; other names are NIJ DHAM, SAT LOK, and SACH KHAND; the first region of pure SPIRIT.

mukti. *MOOK-tee* Salvation here and now. *See also* JIVAN MUKTI; MOKSHA.

muladhara chakra. *See* ADHAR CHAKRA, MULCHAKRA.

mulchakra. *mool-CHAH-krah* The four-petaled CHAKRA, or microcosmic center, in the body near the rectum, which governs elimination; also called muladhara or guda chakra. *See also* ADHAR CHAKRA, MICROCOSMIC CENTERS.

mumukshutwa. *moo-mook-SHOOT-wah* The state of attainment; or one who desires to attain MOKSHA, or salvation from the rounds of births and DEATHS.

muni. *MOO-nee* A sage or RISHI.

Mursheed. *moor-SHEED* A master among the Muslims and Sufis; often applied to those who are neither saints nor masters.

music and ECK. The AUDIBLE LIFE STREAM is the origin of all melodies in the universes of the world; the ECK is transposed by the musician from the inner to the outer senses.

musical life current. The sublime music, the spiritual food of the SOUND CURRENT, without which nothing could live or exist, which fills all space and rings with far more enchanting music through all the higher worlds.

music of the spheres. The music of the SUGMAD; the ECK; the BANI; the HU; the WORD; the SHABDA; the QUALIMA; the Nad, or that music which can only be heard with the INNER EARS of SOUL.

Muzuart. *MOO-zoo-ahrt* The twelfth twelve-year cycle of the DUO-DENARY CYCLE called the Years of the Trembling Leaf. *See also* CYCLES OF TWELVE.

mystery schools. Groups gathered under the guiding hand of a master, or teacher of the spiritual truths, who revealed the mysteries of nature; out of the great religions have come varied mystery groups of modern times.

mystical marriage. Realization of the true relationship between SPIRIT and the individual CONSCIOUSNESS; the two have ceased to be separate and have become one.

M

N

Naacal Records. *NAH-kahl* The first known records of mankind which are the writings of the third ROOT RACE, the LEMURIANS; YUONT-NA, a teacher of ECK and total CONSCIOUSNESS, is mentioned in them; they are kept at the KATSUPARI MONASTERY in Tibet under the guardianship of the ECK MASTERS.

nabhi chakra. *NAHB-ee CHAH-krah* The third microcosmic center in the body, located near the solar plexus, which has to do mostly with nutrition; often called ASHTA-DAL-KANWAL, it has eight petals. *See also* CHAKRA(s); MICROCOSMIC CENTERS.

Nada. *NAH-dah* Also Nad. The word for the SOUND CURRENT used in the VEDAS; another word for ECK, the MUSIC OF THE SPHERES; the whole of the visible and invisible universe is the MANIFESTATION of the primal Nada.

Nada Bindu. *NAH-dah BIN-doo* The Sound from which all things grow; the seed Sound, the ECK; a SECRET WORD used by the ADEPTS for the growth of a CHELA; used for spiritual or physical growth; the BANI.

Nada Brahm. *NAH-dah BRAHM* The PRIMAL WORD of BRAHM; the creative Sound, that CREATIVE ENERGY; the primal music of the universe; by It all CREATION was brought into existence; the grand symphony out of which all other symphonies flow in everything below the BRAHM LOK; the voice of the Supreme CREATOR.

naijor-pa. *NIE-johr-PAH* One who attains serenity.

103

Nalpa Keljina. *NAHL-pah kehl-JEE-nah* The Living ECK Master who lived in Greece during the time of the Trojan War, 1200 B.C.

Nam. *NAHM* The word of the INITIATION; the word that issues from the heart of God; what God says or does; the Divine Being in action; the living ECK or the living Word.

Namayatan. *nah-mah-YAH-tahn* The Temple of Golden Wisdom in the city of Mer Kailash on the Mental Plane.

Nameless Plane. The Anami Lok, the tenth plane; the world of the Supreme Being, the highest of all beings; the center of the universes.

namo. *NAH-moh* Blessings.

Nampak. *NAHM-pahk* Located in Africa, it is one of the seven SPIRITUAL CITIES which are on earth to help the world.

narrow way. The opening at the top of the head; the name given to the small door there, where Soul enters and leaves the body; spiritual AWARENESS occurs through this opening; the disciplines suggested by the Living ECK Master for the CHELAS.

Nature, or Matter, Ray. The tenth of the ten forces, or rays, of the ECK which are sent out to the worlds below by the SUGMAD through the ECK.

negative. *See* Kal Niranjan; POSITIVE AND NEGATIVE.

neophyte. An ASPIRANT; a beginner in the ECK spiritual works.

Neralit. *neh-rah-LEET* The tenth twelve-year cycle of the DUODE-NARY CYCLE, called the Years of the Raging Fires. *See also* CYCLES OF TWELVE.

neti. *NEH-tee* Not this.

nibbuta. *ni-BOO-tah* The stage of life when the fires of GREED, hate, VANITY, ATTACHMENT, and other passions have been extinguished; beyond all egoistic DESIRES and illusions.

nidanas. *nee-DAHN-ahz* The causes that move each individual SOUL to reincarnate; the twelve ECK-VIDYA signs, or cycles of transmigratory existence, each of which contains within it an impulse to action, or a cause that brings Soul back again into this world.

Nij Dham. *neej DAHM* The FAR COUNTRY; region of pure SPIRIT; SAT DESHA, true country; another name for SACH KHAND, SAT LOK. *See also* MUKAM TAQ.

Nij Manas. *neej MAH-nahz* The inner MIND; carries the seeds of all actions within itself; also carries the SANSKARAS (impressions of all former lives); the CAUSAL BODY; similar to the Universal Mind force.

Nij mind. The true MIND. *See also* KARAN MIND.

nimbus. A circle, or disc, of rays invisible to the senses but perceptible in the INNER VISION, which surrounds the head and body; the AURA.

nimitta. *nee-MEET-tah* The primary cause.

Nine Silent Ones. The nine unknown ECK MASTERS who are responsible for the sacred books of the SHARIYAT-KI-SUGMAD.

nine steps. The stages of spiritual development, or INITIATIONS, through which an ECKIST goes on the path to becoming a CO-WORKER with God.

nirala. *NEE-rah-lah* Peerless; having none like him.

Niranjan. *nee-RAHN-jahn* The negative power in the lower universe. *See also* KAL NIRANJAN.

Niranjan, Jot. *See* JOT NIRANJAN.

Niranjan, Kal. *See* KAL NIRANJAN.

nirankar. *nee-RAHN-kahr* Without body or form; the formless one, without personality; without name; impersonal; the SUGMAD.

nirat. *nee-RAHT* The LIGHT; ECK spiritual exercise wherein one looks for the Light.

niraya. *nee-RAH-yah* The downward path.

Nirgin Sarup. *NEER-geen sah-ROOP* The true body of the SUGMAD; the OCEAN OF LOVE AND MERCY.

Nirguna. *neer-GOO-nah* The inside of the SUGMAD which has no qualities, and nothing can be said or thought about IT; the NO-THING self. *See also* SAGUNA; SUGMAD.

Nirguna Ekam. *neer-GOO-nah EHK-ahm* An ECK MASTER who is one of the guardians of the SHARIYAT-KI-SUGMAD at the Temple of PARAM AKSHAR on the SOUL PLANE.

nirmala charan. *neer-MAH-lah chah-RAHN* The waters of IM-MORTALITY; the fountain of youth, or spring of pure water, in the HIMALAYAS close to the headwaters of the Jhelum river.

nirvana. *neer-VAH-nah* Heaven for the Buddhist; the Fourth Plane. *See also* MENTAL PLANE.

Nirvikalpa. *neer-vee-KAHL-pah* A spiritual state of CONSCIOUS-NESS; belongs in the area of the true ECK worlds; leads to DETACHMENT, which eventually takes the CHELA through the varied INITIATIONS into the Ninth, when he becomes a candidate for possible entry into the Order of the Vairagi, the ECK MASTERS; a state of GOD CONSCIOUSNESS. *See also* GOD-REALIZATION.

nirvretti. *neer-VREH-tee* Returning; going back; flow-back.

Niyamg. *nee-YAHMG* The twelfth month of the ECK-VIDYA calendar, December, called the month of the onyx, or the days of CHARITY. *See also* JOURNEY OF SOUL.

niyana. *nee-YAH-nah* Self-restrained.

no-thing. The nothingness of the SUGMAD; the nothingness that is everything; that which is not energy, matter, space, or time; the world within; the power of knowing, INTUITION, or instinctive knowledge is connected to the no-thing universe.

nowness of the SUGMAD. The present moment; BEINGNESS of truth; isness and hereness of the SUGMAD; a stillness of motion; the extension of the creative moment into lengths; the preservation of the moment. *See also* SUGMAD TRINITY.

Nukti-i-saveda. *NOOK-tee-ee-sah-VAY-dah* The SHIVA-NETRA, the eye of SHIVA; the black point in the circle, the naught; the lefthand path of black MAGIC; the concentration that keeps SOUL earthbound; use of the SPIRITUAL EYE backwards.

numbers, doctrine of. *See* DOCTRINE OF NUMBERS.

Nuri. *NOO-ree* LIGHT, or LIGHT BODY; ASTRAL BODY.

Nuri Rupa. *See* NURI SARUP.

Nuri Sarup. *NOO-ree sah-ROOP* The LIGHT BODY of the ASTRAL WORLD; through this body the MIND and SOUL communicate with the PHYSICAL BODY; the inner form of the LIVING ECK MASTER; his Light form.

N

O

Ocean of Love and Mercy. The SUGMAD, God; IT projects IT-SELF in the form of waves emerging out of a fountain; since It contains the qualities of the SUGMAD, It can only appear on the LOWER PLANES, including the physical, as the form of CONSCIOUS-NESS; the ECK is the ocean of life, a life-giving, creative sea, and is heard by the divine followers of the SUGMAD; within the ocean of love is the total sum of all teachings emanating from the SUGMAD; It is the divine word, for It includes everything IT has said or done.

om. *See* AUM.

Omar Khayyam. *OH-mahr kah-YAHM* A Persian poet of the twelfth century who was an advocate of ECK.

Omkar. *OHM-kahr* The power of the negative on the MENTAL PLANE, or the region of the Universal Mind.

omnipotence. All-powerful; BEINGNESS of all power, the SUGMAD.

omnipotent law. The all-powerful nature of the LIVING ECK MASTER is the fundamental basis of all things.

omnipresence. Present in all things; BEINGNESS of all things; the SUGMAD.

omniscience. All-knowing; TOTAL AWARENESS; the SUGMAD.

ontology. The science of BEING or reality; the branch of knowledge that investigates the nature, essential properties, and relations of being.

onyx, month of the. *See* JOURNEY OF SOUL; NIYAMG.

opal, month of the. *See* EBKIA; JOURNEY OF SOUL.

Opposites, Law of. *See* POLARITY, LAW OF.

oracles. Famous shrines where the future was predicted by the chief priest or an enlightened being. *See also* TIRMER, ORACLE OF.

Order of the Vairagi. *See* VAIRAGI ADEPTS.

Ori Diogo. *OH-ree dee-OH-goh* The LIVING ECK MASTER during the time of Julius Caesar, who foretold the DEATH of Caesar; he is in charge of healing on the ASTRAL PLANE.

ormad. *ohr-MAHD* Illumination.

Orpheus. *OHR-fee-uhs* A musician who was a student in the ECK MYSTERY SCHOOLS; the Orphic mystery school came out of his teachings.

Osiris. *oh-SEE-ris* One of the ways the MAHANTA Consciousness as the vehicle for the SUGMAD appeared to the Egyptians; It also appeared as their Amun Re and Aton.

Ousia. *OO-see-ah* The spiritual ESSENCE that flows out of the GOD-HEAD; the ECK.

Outer Master. *See* LIVING ECK MASTER.

oversoul. The DIVINE ESSENCE; the SUGMAD; God.

P

pad. *PAHD* Plane, station, or place.

Padma Gaya. *PAHD-mah GAH-yah* The LIVING ECK MASTER at Nineveh when it was destroyed by the Babylonians in 612 B.C., who was present at the building of the Hanging Gardens by Nebuchadnezzar as well as the destruction of King Solomon's Temple.

Padma Samba. *PAHD-mah SAHM-bah* The title of the ECK MASTER who is the guardian of the SHARIYAT-KI-SUGMAD, the holy book of ECK in the SATA VISIC PALACE, the TEMPLE OF GOLDEN WISDOM, on the ANAMI LOK, the tenth plane of the God Worlds of ECK.

pamada. *pah-MAH-dah* Mental slowness; sloth of MIND.

pantheism. The doctrine that God is everything and everything is God; the worship of all gods.

panthi. *PAHN-thee* One who travels the path of God.

par. *PAHR* Beyond the material or psychic worlds; in the SPIRITUAL WORLDS.

Para Atma. *PAH-rah AHT-mah* The Hindu name for the true reality, the SUGMAD, the ultimate, God.

Para Atman. *PAH-rah AHT-mahn* The great SPIRIT; the ECK.

Parabrahm. *pah-rah-BRAHM* Above the BRAHM, or MENTAL PLANE; a very thin world between the Mental and SOUL planes; the ETHERIC PLANE; the title of the ruler of this plane.

Param Akshar. *PAH-rahm AHK-shahr* The TEMPLE OF GOLDEN WISDOM, the HOUSE OF IMPERISHABLE KNOWLEDGE, on the SOUL PLANE, the ATMA LOK; Supreme Lord; another name for God.

Paramhansas. *pah-rahm-HAHN-sahz* Also Parahansas or Paramahansas. One who has reached the plane of SAT NAM, the SOUL PLANE, is like a swan; *hansa* means swan, a bird of beauty and cleanliness.

Param Mahanta. *PAH-rahm mah-HAHN-tah* The supreme one; the SAT GURU; the LIGHT bearer for this physical universe; the true SPIRITUAL MASTER.

Param Sant. *PAH-rahm SAHNT* One who has reached the state of CONSCIOUSNESS of a saint who is able to reach the region of SAT NAM and travel into the worlds above the Fifth Plane.

paranirvana. *PAH-rah-neer-VAH-nah* Beyond NIRVANA.

Para Vidya. *PAH-rah VEE-dyah* Self-knowledge; SELF-REALIZATION; spiritual knowledge of the objective world—like the knowledge of the VEDAS, ASTROLOGY, conduct, morals, and ethics.

Par Brahm. *PAHR BRAHM* The Lord of the MENTAL PLANE, or MAHA KAL LOK, whose duties are to make all seekers of God believe this is the top of the worlds, the final resting place.

par ECK. *PAHR EHK* The INITIATION on the ETHERIC, or PARABRAHM, PLANE.

Parinama. *pah-ree-NAH-mah* The tenth month of the ECK-VIDYA calendar, October, called the days of beauty, the month of the jasper. The quiet period in the journey of SOUL, where It strives for the common good; not for glory, but for honor. *See* JOURNEY OF SOUL.

passions of the mind. *See* FIVE PASSIONS OF THE MIND.

path of Soul. To contemplate the life, love, and beauty of DIVINE POWER, of the LIGHT AND SOUND, and to affirm Itself as already giving expression of It as a CHANNEL, in thought, feeling, and action; it is neither positive nor negative, but is the movement of CONSCIOUSNESS of SOUL.

path of the trinity. Three questions to ask oneself when in doubt about an action: Is it true? Is it necessary? Is it kind?

patience. Enduring with calmness and self-control with the MIND steadfast upon the LIGHT of God; attention to the goal of GOD-REALIZATION; the greatest discipline in all the works of ECK.

Paulji. *PAHL-jee* A title of love and respect for PAUL TWITCHELL. *See also* TWITCHELL, PAUL; PEDDAR ZASKQ.

pearl, month of the. *See* HORTAR; JOURNEY OF SOUL.

Peddar Zaskq. *PEH-dahr ZASK* The true spiritual name for PAUL TWITCHELL, the MAHANTA and LIVING ECK MASTER from 1965 to 1971. *See also* PAULJI; TWITCHELL, PAUL.

perversions of the mind. *See* FIVE PASSIONS OF THE MIND.

phenomena. *See* PSYCHIC PHENOMENA.

philosophy. A study of the causes of life by the use of the INTELLECT.

philosophy of ECKANKAR. That branch of the ECK SOUND CURRENT which embraces the science comprising ethics, aesthetics, metaphysics, and the knowledge of the underlying principles of the trinity: WISDOM, power, and freedom.

physical body. The body SOUL operates on the PHYSICAL PLANE.

Physical Plane. The physical universe; the region of the illusion of reality (MAYA), science, PHYSICAL BODIES, day-to-day events in life; the first step on the road to the secret kingdom; the sound is thunder, and the word is ALAYI; the plane of matter, energy, time, and space.

113

Physical Ray. The ninth of the ten forces, or rays, of the ECK which are sent out to the worlds below by the SUGMAD through the ECK.

pinda. *PIN-dah* Also pindi. Represents the PHYSICAL BODY of man and corresponds with the thousand-petaled lotus in the physical body; the Hindu word for the PHYSICAL PLANE, or universe.

Pinda Lok. *See* PHYSICAL PLANE.

pinda mind. *PIN-dah* One of the parts of MIND, the lower-world mind; the term used for the part of mind acting on the PHYSICAL PLANE. *See also* MIND.

Pinda Sarup. *PIN-dah sah-ROOP* The PHYSICAL BODY.

pingala. *pin-GAH-lah* Pingala is the channel at the left side of the spine, to the left of the central canal; IDA is the channel to the right, in the SUBTLE BODY; the sushumna path of the occultist, through which the psychic force, or KUNDALINI, rises.

Piscean Age. A two-thousand-year era which ended in March, 1948; it has been followed by the Aquarian Age, which is still under the darkness of the KALI YUGA.

piti. *PEE-tee* Rapture.

planes. The mystic lands through which SOUL must travel on Its way back to the OCEAN OF LOVE AND MERCY, the GODHEAD; the twelve steps on the spiritual path to the SUGMAD; there are an infinite number which blend and shift from one state to another. *See also* LOWER PLANES; SPIRITUAL WORLDS.

Polarians. The first ROOT RACE which lived in Polara, the GARDEN OF EDEN; ADOM was the first man and EDE, the first woman; the beginning of the races of man upon earth.

Polarity, Law of. The Law of Opposites. The third law of the physical universe; the state of opposition between any two related factors; yin and yang (negative and positive), feminine and masculine; the negative, or reactive, side and the positive, or active side; the third part is the passive, or middle, path; each thing within this universe is supported, animated, maintained by, and in opposition to its opposite.

polarity of Soul. When SOUL is aligned or polarized in either the GODHEAD or the KAL (negative).

polytheism. Many gods.

Popul Vuh, The. *POH-pool VUH* An ancient historical work.

positive and negative. The positive is the outgoing, the God force; the negative is the inert, receptive force; the positive is forever transforming into the negative and the negative is forever in the process of becoming the positive; without one the other could not exist.

power. The force of ECK that manifests as negative or positive in the lower worlds and as a spiritual force in the higher planes.

Power Ray. The second of the ten forces, or rays, of the ECK which are sent out to the worlds below by the SUGMAD through the ECK.

praabdh karma. *PRAHB-duh KAR-mah* Also prarabdh karma; fate karma; that which has been earned in one or more previous lives, and upon which this present life is based; must be met and paid for by the individual.

prabhswami. *prahb-SWAH-mee* All-pervading lord, having power.

prabhu. *PRAHB-hoo* Lord, having power and control.

Prada Vidya. *PRAH-dah VEE-dyah* GOD-REALIZATION; beyond the sense world; the knowledge of God; he who has God-Realization is released from the bondage of all things.

pradhana. *prahd-HAH-nah* The primary matter of SPIRIT; the nature stuff.

Prajapati. *prah-jah-PAH-tee* The ECK MASTER who cares for animals.

prakriti. *PRAH-kree-tee* Nature; the KAL force; substance, as opposed to the ECK (SPIRIT).

pralaya. *prah-LAH-yah* The dissolution and reabsorption of the universes of the lower worlds at the end of each KALPA, and the time of the formation of a new universe in the bosom of the SUGMAD.

pralobdh. *prah-LOHB-duh* Means destiny.

pralobd karma. *See* PRAABDH KARMA.

prana. *PRAH-nah* The SANSKRIT word for the DIVINE POWER; the Oriental term for that which the physical scientists call energy. It is only a MANIFESTATION of the audible SOUND CURRENT stepped down to meet material conditions; breath, vital air; the plastic ether.

Pranava. *prah-NAH-vah* The same as OMKAR, the ruler of the MENTAL PLANE.

Prapatti Marg. *prah-PAH-tee MAHRG* Way of liberation by complete surrender and devotion to God via the Master.

prathiba. *praht-HEE-bah* A degree of illumination which comes as a result of purity alone, or one who was born to this state as the supreme genius, the great poet, the superb artist, the philanthropist, etc.

pratyahara. *praht-yah-HAH-rah* The practice of complete withdrawal of CONSCIOUSNESS from the environment.

prescience. Foreknowledge.

pret. *PREHT* One of the hosts of beings in the subtle region close to the earth who have great powers and are quite willing to serve people who live in harmony with them; somewhat above ordinary man, they help to serve him in many ways.

primal energy. A modified form of the SOUND CURRENT, the dynamic, CREATIVE FORCE, the ECK.

primal matter force. *See* AKASHA.

primal Sound. The ECK; CREATIVE ENERGY; the DIVINE VOICE, out of which all other sounds flow.

primal Vadan. *See* VADAN.

primal Word. That which gives the life substance to all things; the SOUND CURRENT; the ECK.

primary states of matter. TATTWAS, elements, or ESSENCES: PRITHVI, earth; JAL, water; VAYU air; AGNI, fire; and AKASH, ether.

principle. Primary cause or universal truth.

principle of ECKANKAR, basic. The world of CREATION is finished, and the original of all things lies within man.

principle of God. All life exists because God so wills it; SOUL exists because of God's love for It.

principle of HU. The original word CURRENT, HU, is the father of all motions, forces, lights, sounds, and elements that subsequently came into existence.

principle of life. The power of the ECK is the life principle of every atom which is in existence; every atom is striving continually to manifest more life; all are intelligent, and all are seeking to carry out the purpose for which they were created.

principle of Soul. No two things can occupy the same space in the lower worlds at the same time, except SOUL.

principles of consciousness, seven. Appreciation, sincerity, unselfishness, idealism, devotion, personal effort, and attainment.

principles of the Godhead. (1) Reality is an all-embracing unity; (2) the Ultimate is nameless; (3) within the Self the Ultimate is to be found; (4) IT can be known by acquaintance; and (5) reality is disclosed only to those who meet ITS conditions.

principles of the universes. The Deity (God or the SUGMAD); the CREATIVE POWER (ECK); and the world-soul (the magnetic field that surrounds all the universes and each universe individually, as well as individual planets, planes, and regions).

Priscus. *PREES-kuhs* The LIVING ECK MASTER who followed KETU JARAUL and was in England at the time of its conquest by William of Normandy; preached support of the First Crusade which he accompanied; he died in the Holy Lands.

prit. *PREET* Positive force; CREATIVE FORCE in man.

prithvi. *PREETH-vee* Also prithva. Earth and related subjects; one of the TATTWAS, the five PRIMARY STATES OF MATTER, the others being JAL, VAYU, AKASH, and AGNI.

Prithvi Lok. *PREETH-vee LOHK* The earth world.

prophecy. The art of foreseeing events before they happen and DEJA VU for seeing what has already happened are the modus operandi of the ECK-VIDYA, the ancient science of prophecy used by the ADEPTS of ECKANKAR.

Protean Soul. *PROH-tee-ahn* Higher form of the ASTRAL BODY used at times by the Master to appear to the CHELA; his thought can force it to assume any shape or form.

P

psychic law. Love is good, and power is bad; not a spiritual subject, but one belonging to the ASTRAL WORLD; not any law of the higher levels of life.

psychic phenomena. Those events which occur in the physical world but cannot be explained by the laws of the physical; the inner experiences which are not of the SOUL PLANE or above; events which are particularly from the ASTRAL PLANE, such as flying saucers, ghosts, etc.

psychic realization. The realization of the intellectual powers and the psychic strength and abilities that come with it; many mistake it for the illumination, or COSMIC CONSCIOUSNESS, which is another degree on the spiritual path; the learning of control over MIND and matter.

psychic space.   The granting to others the right to be themselves, and by this granting, to be free oneself.

psychic worlds.   Also psychic PLANES. The four planes which correspond to the spinal centers below the neck (psychic worlds of the CHAKRAS); each plane has a ruler and there is a body for each; these lower worlds are the PHYSICAL, ASTRAL, CAUSAL, and MENTAL PLANES.

punya.   *POON-yah*   Spiritual merit; CHARITY (love).

purification.   Breaking the fixed DESIRES of the basic nature and making contact with the God power; to relax in God and let ITS blessings flow.

Purusha.   *poo-ROO-shah*   The male, supreme CREATIVE ENERGY; implies BEING and being implies creative energy; the presiding and predominating lord; the source of creative energy.

Purushottama.   *poo-roo-SHAH-tah-mah*   The ECK; that wave flowing out of the OCEAN OF LOVE AND MERCY; the supreme CREATIVE ENERGY; the spiritual power.

Pythagoras.   *pi-THAG-ehr-uhs*   An ECK MASTER In the sixth century B.C. who was an ADEPT in the Ancient Order of the Vairagi and was well known as a Greek philosopher.

Pythagoreans.   *pi-thag-uh-REE-ahnz*   The followers of PYTHAGORAS.

P

Q

Qualima. *kwah-LEE-mah* ABSOLUTE TRUTH; the divine melody, the name, the WORD, the ECK, MUSIC OF THE SPHERES; Nad. *See also* NADA.

quality of Soul. Space or no-thingness; It exists everywhere, and has no limitation.

Quetzalcoatl. *keht-sahl-koh-AH-tohl* The Mexican god; an ECK Master who was one of the spiritual teachers of PEDDAR ZASKQ; one of the saviors who was crucified.

quiddity. The ESSENCE; that which makes up the ECK.

quinbodies. Also Quintan. The vehicles used by the MAHANTA which are the PHYSICAL, ASTRAL, CAUSAL, MENTAL, and SOUL BODIES; the word made flesh in the lower worlds, which function as the instruments of God upon each plane throughout the worlds of SPIRIT, including the true spiritual PLANES.

121

R

Rabjung. *rahb-YUHNG* The sixty-year cycle of the ECK-VIDYA system; used for the natal divination of the individual from birth to the grave. *See also* LHOKOR.

Radiant body. The ATMA SARUP or the NURI SARUP, the LIGHT BODY of the MAHANTA, the LIVING ECK MASTER which appears on the inner to those who follow his teachings.

Rahakaz. *rah-hah-KAHZ* A spiritual city at Land's End in Cornwall, England; the legendary Camelot; home of the Order of the Golden Dawn. *See also* SPIRITUAL CITIES.

rajas. *RAH-jahs* Motion; one of the three GUNAS or aspects of the Universal Mind Power. The others are SATTVA, light; and TAMAS, darkness.

Ralot. *rah-LOHT* The fifth month of the ECK-VIDYA calendar, May, the month of the sapphire, the days of truth; the JOURNEY OF SOUL where there is a need for the outward MANIFESTATION of Its inner search.

Rama. *RAH-mah* The first world savior who brought the word of ECK into India, and later to the ARYANS, the fifth ROOT RACE; he was the founder of the KATSUPARI MONASTERY in Tibet.

Rami Nuri. *RAH-mee NOO-ree* The ECK MASTER who is the guardian of the holy book, the SHARIYAT-KI-SUGMAD on the PINDA LOK, the physical world, at the HOUSE OF MOKSHA, TEMPLE OF GOLDEN WISDOM in the city of RETZ, VENUS.

R

Ramkar. *rahm-KAR* Also Ramchar. The lord of the third plane, the CAUSAL PLANE; the power supply station for all the worlds below.

Ra Mu. *rah MOO* The emperor of MU, or LEMURIA, the Empire of the Sun, who was the representative of the Supreme Deity for the LEMURIANS, but was not worshiped by them.

rasayon. *rah-sah-YOHN* The elixir of life.

rays of light. *See* AMESHA SPENTAS.

reality. *See* DIVINE REALITY.

realization. *See* GOD CONSCIOUSNESS; GOD-REALIZATION; SELF-REALIZATION.

Realization Ray. The sixth of the ten forces, or rays, of the ECK which are sent out to the worlds below by the SUGMAD through the ECK.

Rebazar Tarzs. *REE-bah-zahr TAHRZ* The torchbearer of ECKANKAR in the lower worlds; the spiritual teacher of many ECK MASTERS including PEDDAR ZASKQ, or PAUL TWITCHELL, to whom he handed the ROD OF ECK POWER in 1965; said to be over five hundred years old, Rebazar Tarzs lives in a hut in the HINDU KUSH mountains and appears to many as he helps the present LIVING ECK MASTER in the works of ECKANKAR.

R

Records of the Kros. *See* KROS, RECORDS OF THE.

Regional ECK Spiritual Aide. An ECK SPIRITUAL AIDE appointed by the LIVING ECK MASTER to serve as his key representative in a designated region. In this high leadership role, the RESA acts as a watcher, listener, and guardian in matters related to the MESSAGE OF ECK. *See also* ECK SPIRITUAL AIDE.

Regnard. *REHG-nahrd* An ECK MASTER of the future who will be the LIVING ECK MASTER during the time the Mongoloid race will be in power.

reincarnation. Rebirth; the coming and going of SOUL into a new body each time It enters into this world. *See also* DOCTRINE OF REINCARNATION.

religions. Offshoots of ECK, the original source of all life; work in the lower STATES OF CONSCIOUSNESS; along with FAITHS and philosophies, they make up the necessary steps to reach the ECK.

retribution. *See* KARMA, LAW OF.

retrocognition. Seeing into the past; knowledge of the past.

Retz. *REHTS* The capital city of the planet VENUS where the SHARIYAT-KI-SUGMAD is kept in the HOUSE OF MOKSHA, TEMPLE OF GOLDEN WISDOM.

Reversed Effort, Law of. The functioning of the IMAGINATION by negation which draws into the external that which one is trying to avoid.

riddle of God. That the supreme SUGMAD is; that IT expresses in the lower worlds as, or through, the ECK, or SPIRIT, which expresses as or through the MAHANTA, the GODMAN, the supreme son, which expresses through the CHELA, the human SOUL, ray, or drop, who descended from the great, boundless ocean of Spirit, the SUGMAD.

righteous law. *See* DANDA.

rishi. *REE-shee* The Oriental title for the sage, or wise man, who follows the growth pattern similar to that of a yogi.

river of God. The river which pervades all the universes, the great spiritual CURRENT flowing out of the throne of God; the ECK.

river of Light. The great circular wave of Light which flows in a continual stream from God; the great spiritual CURRENT flowing to all the worlds upon worlds; the ECK. *See also* RIVER OF GOD.

Rock of Zin. *ZEEN* The rock struck by Moses from which the water flowed; literal understanding (the stone) struck by the

IMAGINATION (the rod of Moses) issues forth the water of psychological meaning to quench the thirst of humanity.

Rod of ECK Power. The power of the WORD of God, which is given to that being who has been chosen by the SUGMAD, as It descends and enters into the new LIVING ECK MASTER; the power which makes him the actual MANIFESTATION of God at the rites, or the INITIATION, of accepting the Rod of ECK Power; the power of the MAHANTA Consciousness.

rook. *ROOK* SPIRIT or SOUL.

root races. The varied races which have occupied the earth in the past; the POLARIANS, the HYPERBOREANS, the LEMURIANS, the ATLANTEANS, and the present race, the ARYANS; and the races which will be in power in the future; the ULEMANS, the SHATIKAYAS, the ARRIANS, the KAISHVITS, the HERACLIANS, the CLEMAINS, and the FRETICRETS—twelve in all.

ruby, month of the. *See* JOURNEY OF SOUL; KAMITOC.

Rukmini Tunnel. *rook-MEE-nee* The tunnel through which one must pass to reach the BHANWAR GUPHA, the MENTAL PLANE, from the DASWAN DWAR, the ETHERIC PLANE.

Rumi. *See* JALAL AD-DIN AR-RUMI.

Runmensi. *roon-MEHN-see* A cave which is an inner experience SOUL goes through on Its upward journey.

R

rupa. *ROO-pah* Form.

S

sacerdotal language. The secret language which was built upon the decimal system; because it was thought the system was received from the higher powers, it was kept secret from the masses.

Sach Khand. *SAHCH KAHND* The Fifth, or Soul, Plane; the true home of Soul; the grand headquarters of all CREATION, and the region of IMMORTALITY; changeless, perfect, and deathless; untouched by dissolution or reconstruction; the world where the ECK SAINTS live. Also refers to the pure positive God Worlds in general.

sacred numbers. Numbers are symbols of DIVINE REALITIES; the key to the ancient views on life and the evolution of the human race, spiritually as well as physically.

sadhaka. *sahd-HAH-kah* A seeker of truth; looker for God.

sadhana. *sahd-HAH-nah* The spiritual effort or quest for God; sometimes used to denote the SPIRITUAL EXERCISES OF ECK.

sadhu. *SAH-doo* One who has reached the CAUSAL PLANE, or only the higher ASTRAL WORLD; higher than a RISHI or a MAHA RISHI; not a saint; second order of the MAHATMAS.

Sagana Sati. *sah-GAH-nah SAH-tee* A form of inducing trance.

Saguna. *sah-GOO-nah* One of the two attributes of the GODHEAD; eternal reality, CONSCIOUSNESS, and joy experienced at

GOD-REALIZATION; the outer side of the SUGMAD. *See also* NIR-GUNA; SUGMAD.

Saguna Brahm. *sah-GOO-nah BRAHM* The ruler of the SAGUNA LOK, the upper division of the MIND plane, or ETHERIC PLANE, who has jurisdiction over all entities and beings living on this plane.

Saguna Lok. *sah-GOO-nah LOHK* The upper division of the MIND world; the ETHERIC PLANE.

Saguna Sati. *sah-GOO-nah SAH-tee* The instant, or direct, technique for SOUL TRAVEL; DIRECT PROJECTION; the ability to move out of the PHYSICAL BODY at will into any of the higher STATES OF CONSCIOUSNESS.

saguna upasova. *sah-GOO-nah oo-PAH-soh-vah* Highest understanding one can have.

Sahaji. *sah-HAH-jee* SOUL TRAVEL, or ECKANKAR, the way of the SOUND CURRENT practiced by the ECK travelers; the oldest system known in the history of mankind.

Sahak. *SAH-hahk* The sixth month of the ECK-VIDYA calendar, June, the month of the moonstone, the days of music; the journey wherein SOUL seeks a resting place where It can work out Its destiny in peace and quiet. *See also* JOURNEY OF SOUL.

Sahasra-dal-Kanwal. *sah-HAHS-rah-dahl-KAHN-wahl* The CROWN CHAKRA, the thousand-petaled lotus; the capital city of the ASTRAL PLANE, and the MOUNTAIN OF LIGHT at the top of the Astral. *See also* ASTRAL CITY.

Sakapori Temple. *sah-kah-POHR-ee* The TEMPLE OF GOLDEN WISDOM on the BRAHMANDA LOK, the Third, or CAUSAL, PLANE, in the city of HONU.

sakhrat. *SAHK-raht* A single emerald which is the base of the mountain of Caf in Muslim mythology.

saktas. *SAHK-tahz* The worshipers of KALI; the lefthand worshipers were the blood cult, and the righthand worshipers were the worshipers of woman; a form of worship which originated in India.

sakti. *SAHK-tee* The worship of SHIVA; the form of pleasure derived from the female organ.

salamanders. *See* ELEMENTALS.

Salokiam. *sah-loh-kee-AHM* The first of four states which a HIGHER INITIATE passes through in this lifetime as he becomes spiritualized through CONTEMPLATION; also signifies the only tie with the lower worlds. In this state SOUL tries to lift Itself into the SPIRITUAL WORLDS with the aid of the MAHANTA, the LIVING ECK MASTER. *See also* SAMIPIAM; SOUAROUPIAM; SAYODIAM.

samadhana. *sah-mah-DAH-nah* A religious state in which joy is felt beyond all doubt.

Samadhi. *sah-MAH-dee* SELF-REALIZATION; a state of CONSCIOUSNESS. *See also* NIRVIKALPA.

samandi. *sah-MAHN-dee* MEDITATION; a form of spiritual petition.

samati. *SAH-mah-tee* Sameness of MIND.

samhita. *sahm-HEE-tah* A code of rules, or laws; similar to the MANU SAMHITA.

Samipiam. *sah-mee-pee-AHM* The second of the four states which the HIGHER INITIATE passes through in this lifetime as he becomes spiritualized; signifies proximity; a state in which SOUL comes closer to the God state and recognizes a marked elevation in consciousness; the disregard of all earthly objects so that the knowledge and idea of the SUGMAD becomes familiar to It. *See also* SALOKIAM; SAYODIAM; SOUAROUPIAM.

S

sampatti. *sahm-PAHT-tee* Wealth or treasure.

samsara. *sahm-SAH-rah* The world of changes which is the psychic universe, the LOWER PLANES.

samyana. *sahm-YAH-nah* Restraints from worldly pleasures.

Sangwa. *sahng-WAH* Secret doctrine or MESSAGE OF ECK.

sanna. *SAH-nah* AWARENESS; perception.

sannyasin. *sahn-NYAH-seen* Anyone who renounces the world; free from ATTACHMENT; a CHELA.

sansar. *sahn-SAHR* The material world.

sansari. *sahn-SAH-ree* A worldly person.

sanskaras. *sahn-SKAH-rahz* Impressions during earthly lives; the impressions of all former lives.

Sanskrit. Ancient language of India; writings include the VEDAS, Upanishads, and the Mahabharata which cannot be traced beyond ten thousand years on this planet; the alphabet consists of fifty-two letters which correspond to the fifty-two petals on the CHAKRAS in the PHYSICAL BODY; the fifty-two sounds of these letters comprise all the sounds which can be made by the vocal organs of man.

sant. *SAHNT* The title of one who is spiritually superior to a RISHI or MAHA RISHI.

santosha. *sahn-TOH-shah* Peace and contentment; SHANTI, the peace of self which comes when one is rid of DESIRE; a step on the path to the FAR COUNTRY; the opposite of KAMA, or LUST.

sapphire, month of the. *See* JOURNEY OF SOUL; RALOT.

Sar. *SAHR* One of the peaks below TIRICH MIR in the HINDU KUSH range.

saran. *sah-RAHN* Unqualified submission.

Sardar Lhunpo. *SAHR-dahr LOON-poh* The LIVING ECK MASTER in Rome during the early years of the Republic; his work is now on the CAUSAL PLANE.

Sar-Kurteva. *SAHR-kuhr-TEH-vah* City in ancient ATLANTIS.

sarup. *sah-ROOP* The ECK word for body.

sastras. *SAHS-trahz* Verses in ECK.

sat. *SAHT* Truth; reality; existence; that which is not sat does not really exist; fundamental idea of truth is existence; the untrue does not exist, the true does.

Sata Visic Palace. *SAH-tah VEE-seek* The TEMPLE OF GOLDEN WISDOM on the ANAMI LOK, the tenth plane of the GOD WORLDS OF ECK, where this section of the SHARIYAT-KI-SUGMAD is kept.

Sat Desha. *SAHT DEH-shah* Also Sat Desh. The pure SPIRITUAL WORLDS of God; the world of BEING; the ANAMI LOK, the grand region of all CREATION and of IMMORTALITY.

Sat Dham. *SAHT DAHM* One of the seven SPIRITUAL CITIES which is on earth to help this world; located in the Pyrenees mountains.

Sat Guru. *SAHT GOO-roo* The son of God; one who is responsible directly to the supreme Deity; the chief spiritual authority who speaks for God on every plane through all the universes from the lowest negative to the highest spiritual one; the LIGHT GIVER; the superior teacher of spiritual works. *See also* LIVING ECK MASTER; MAHANTA.

Sat Kanwal-Anda Lok. *SAHT KAHN-wahl-AHN-dah LOHK* The second plane, which is the ASTRAL, or the emotional, world. *See also* ANDA LOK.

Sat Lok. *SAHT LOHK* The Fifth, or SOUL, PLANE; the first step of SOUL into the worlds of God. *See also* ATMA LOK.

Sat Nam. *SAHT NAHM* True name; the ruler of the Fifth Plane, and the first MANIFESTATION of God; the lord of all above and below; the power, the light, flowing down and out into all CREATION, to create, govern and sustain all regions, like a gigantic stream of water.

Sato Kuraj. *SAH-toh KOO-raj* An ECK MASTER who is the guardian of the book of the ECK Masters, the SHARIYAT-KI-SUGMAD, in the HALL OF BRAHMANDA, on the MENTAL PLANE.

satori. *sah-TOH-ree* ENLIGHTENMENT; to transcend the flesh and become reawakened in the spirit.

Sat Purusha. *SAHT poo-ROO-shah* True being; true CREATIVE ENERGY; the predominating and presiding Lord; the source of creative energy; SAT NAM.

Satsang. *SAHT-sahng* Union with that which is pure and imperishable; *sat* means "true" or "unchangeable," *sang* means "union," the coming in contact of man with the LIVING ECK MASTER; study of the works of ECK; company of the Living ECK Master or one of the higher DEVOTEES: hearing or reading the discourses of the Master: going in and making contact with the ECK SOUND CURRENT; the union of one with the Living ECK Master; a spiritual gathering in the name of the ECK. *See also* ECK SATSANG.

Satsangi. *saht-SAHN-gee* A follower of the Master; one who has been initiated and attends SATSANG meetings.

sattva. *SAHT-vah* SANSKRIT for the ethereal substance which is one of the parts of the SOUND CURRENT. Also, the name for one of the three GUNAS (qualities of MIND) of Yoga and Vedanta philosophy.

Satya Yuga. *SAHT-yah YOO-gah* The first era, or Golden Age, of this CREATION; one of four CYCLES OF TIME called YUGAS (ages) which comprise a day of God; the first four tenths, or 1,728,000 years, of that time. *See also* MANVANTARA.

savior gods. The MAHANTA Consciousness manifesting physically to different races at different periods of human history as the vehicle for the SUGMAD in the form to which they were most accustomed and by the name familiar to them, such as Zeus to the Greeks, JUPITER to the Romans, JESUS to the Christians, ALLAH to the Muhammadans, etc.

Sayodiyam. *sah-yoh-dee-YAHM* The fourth of the four states which the HIGHER INITIATE passes through in this lifetime as he becomes spiritualized: where SOUL becomes closely united with the MAHANTA, the LIVING ECK MASTER at the DEATH of the PHYSICAL BODY. *See also* SALOKIAM; SAMIPIAM; SOUAROUPIAM.

Second Grand Division. In literature referring to two grand divisions, the Second Grand Division is the PLANES of the SUGMAD above the lower worlds.

secret word. The holy ECK, or the word given to the CHELA at the time of INITIATION, which must be practiced in silence or vocally only when alone.

seed body. *See* BIJ SHARIR.

seekers of truth. Those who search for the ESSENCE, SPIRIT, SOUL, Itself unchangeable and immortal; those who sincerely work at any sacrifice to attain truth.

self-awareness. *See* SELF-REALIZATION.

Self-determination Ray. The seventh of the ten forces, or rays, of the ECK which are sent out to the worlds below by the SUGMAD through the ECK.

self-discipline. The control of the subjective self; control of the emotional feelings and the imaginative forces.

self-identity. That aspect by which man recognizes himself as being a separate entity from the crowd; one of the steps on the path to the SUGMAD.

Self-Realization. The entering of SOUL into the SOUL PLANE, the first plane of the heavenly country, and there beholding Itself as pure SPIRIT, stripped of all materiality; Soul recognition on the Fifth, or ATMA, Plane.

self-surrender. Submission to the INNER MASTER in all areas of life both physical and spiritual, and devotion to the ECK; concentrated love for the Master of MIND, heart, and will; love of the Master which is greater than anything else; being so completely interested in the Inner Master that nothing else matters.

Seltea. *SEHL-tee-ah* The eighth twelve-year cycle of the DUODE-NARY CYCLE in the study of the ECK-VIDYA cycles called the Years of the Bountiful Earth. *See also* CYCLES OF TWELVE.

Sepher. *SEHP-hehr* The ECK MASTER who will be responsible for the spiritual welfare of the ZOHAR PEOPLE, the seventh ROOT RACE who will colonize the earth after the catastrophe in the twenty-first and twenty-second centuries.

Seres. *SEER-eez* A mighty host of beings from the ASTRAL PLANE who explored the lower worlds leaving traces on earth; the fathering tribe of the LEMURIANS and ATLANTEANS; they had superior knowledge and occult powers.

sewa. *SAY-wah* Service to or for the Master.

Shab. *SHAHB* The lover of life; the INITIATE of the Seventh Circle of ECKANKAR who is also known as the BHAKTI.

Shabda. *SHAHB-dah* The Voice of the SUGMAD as the vibration of the SUGMAD, ITSELF; the Sound; the ECK.

Shabda Dhun. *SHAHB-dah DOON* One of the names of the Voice that is the ESSENCE, the Holy Ghost, the Comforter, the DIVINE SPIRIT that gives life to all; the ECK.

Shabda-Mahanta. *SHAHB-dah-mah-HAHN-tah* One of the two modes of CONTEMPLATION; communication on the inner with the MAHANTA Consciousness. *See also* SHABDA-SUGMAD.

Shabda-SUGMAD. *SHAHB-dah-SOOG-mahd* One of the two modes of CONTEMPLATION; communication on the inner with the SUGMAD. *See also* SHABDA-MAHANTA.

Shabda Yoga. *SHAHB-dah YOH-gah* A group formed out of ECK; a variation of the system of ECK.

Shakti. *SHAHK-tee* The female counterpart of BRAHM, or the KAL NIRANJAN; represents a minor CREATIVE CURRENT; in the Hindu religion, the mother of BRAHMA, VISHNU, and SHIVA.

Shamballa. *shahm-BAH-lah* One of the seven spiritual cities which help this world, located in India.

Shamus-i-Tabriz. *SHAH-muhs-ee-tah-BREEZ* The ADEPT and guardian of the SHARIYAT-KI-SUGMAD in the Temple of SAKAPORI on the CAUSAL PLANE; the teacherof JALAL AD-DIN UD-RUMI, thirteenth-century Persian poet, sage, and a follower of ECK.

Shandava. *shahn-DAH-vah* An ECK ADEPT who dwells on the SOUL PLANE.

shanti. *SHAHN-tee* Peace in the Hindu language; peace of mind; the CHANT for the Sixth Plane, or ALAKH LOK.

Shariat. *shah-ree-AHT* A stage of spiritual unfoldment where rules are needed for the external mode of religious life.

Shariyat-Ki-Sugmad. *SHAH-ree-aht-kee-SOOG-mahd* WAY OF THE ETERNAL; the holy scriptures of ECK; a section is located at each of the various TEMPLES OF GOLDEN WISDOM on the different PLANES, including the earth world, guarded by a particular ECK MASTER, who is also the preceptor of these sacred writings which are under him; CHELAS of ECKANKAR are taken in the DREAM STATE to study these great scriptures.

Shat-dal. *SHAHT-dahl* Offshoot of the KALI CURRENT; sometimes called the daughter of Kali.

Shat-dal-Kanwal. *See* INDRI CHAKRA.

Shat-das-dal-Kanwal. *See* KANTH CHAKRA.

Shatikayas. *shah-tee-KAY-yahs* A fierce, warlike tribe whose ancestors were the warrior tribes of old India; they will come out of the Shatikaya continent which will form during the upheaval when parts of the present world will sink and land masses break up around the year 2500 A.D.

S

Shiva. *SHEE-vah* One of the three CURRENTS flowing out of the BRAHM LOK world; the current of destruction. *See also* TRINITY OF THE HINDUS.

Shiva-netra. *SHEE-vah-NEH-trah* The eye of SHIVA, the THIRD EYE; the four-petaled lotus center in the CHAKRA which is located between the eyebrows. *See also* TISRA TIL.

135

Shiv Sena. *SHEEV SEH-nah* The LIVING ECK MASTER who followed MORAJI DESAI; the Hindu who inspired Moses to lead the Israelites out of Egypt, opened up the Red Sea, and advised Moses to go to the mountain where the Ten Commandments were revealed; he is now on the Fifth Plane working under the deity, SAT NAM.

Shottama. *shoht-TAH-mah* The imaginary image and the energy by which SOUL has the power to act; It is Its own power, created out of the universal SOUND CURRENT, the invisible thread of life upon which Soul travels.

Shraddha. *SHRAHD-dah* The INITIATE of the Sixth Circle, which is the ALAKH LOK, the sixth plane, or step, on the path of ECKANKAR.

siddhis. *SEED-deez* Psychic powers, spiritual powers, supernormal powers, prophecy, healing, etc.

Silence, Law of. *See* KAMIT.

Silent Ones. *See* MAHAVAKYIS.

Silver Age. *See* TRETYA YUGA.

silver cord. The communication line which is attached to each of the varied bodies which SOUL carries with It regularly, except for the SOUL BODY (ATMA SARUP); the line which holds the material bodies to the various PLANES: PHYSICAL, ASTRAL, CAUSAL, and MENTAL.

S

Simha. *SEEM-hah* The lady of ECK, who is considered to be the mother of all ECK MASTERS born in the world of matter.

simran. *SEEM-rahn* Repetition of the holy names of God.

sinchit karma. *SEEN-cheet KAR-mah* Reserve karma; drawn upon at the will of the LORDS OF KARMA, and not by the will of the individual. *See also* KARMA, LAW OF.

sixty-year cycle. *See* RABJUNG.

skandhas. *SKAHN-dahz* Ideas, wishes, DREAMS, and CONSCIOUS-NESS of the lower self which create ATTACHMENTS to the physical realm. *See also* ATTACHMENT.

smarana. *smah-RAH-nah* The repeating of holy names.

soami. *See* SWAMI.

Socrates. A Greek philosopher of the fifth century B.C. who was taught ECK by the ancient Adepts.

Sohang ECK. *SOH-hahng EHK* The sound like that of a keen flute which is heard on the Fourth Plane, the BHANWAR GUPHA.

Sohang, Lord. *SOH-hahng* The Lord of the land of BHANWAR GUPHA, the ETHERIC PLANE; the great power CURRENT flows through him into this region and downward; the name means "I am that!"

Sokagampo. *soh-kah-GAHM-poh* The title of the guardian of the holy book of ECKANKAR, the SHARIYAT-KI-SUGMAD, at the TAMANATA KOP TEMPLE OF GOLDEN WISDOM on the ALAKH LOK, the sixth plane. This is currently TOMO GESHIG.

soma. *SOH-mah* A Hindu beverage, on the order of the Greek ambrosia or nectar, quaffed by initiated Brahmans in order to reach heaven.

Souaroupiam. *swah-roo-pee-YAHM* The third of the four states through which the HIGHER INITIATE must pass in this lifetime as he becomes spiritualized; signifies resemblance; the gradual acquisition of a perfect resemblance to the ECK and participation in all Its attributes. *See also* SALOKIAM; SAMIPIAM; SAYODIYAM.

Soul. That which has no form, no movement, no location in the world of time and space, but has the ability to know, see, hear, and perceive; that is, has perception, opinions, and the ability to assume, or claim, a position in life's work, or the SPIRITUAL WORLDS; the creative center of Its own world. *See also* ATMA; BEINGNESS.

Soul body. The ATMA SARUP, or ATMA SHARIR, the body in which SOUL dwells on the Fifth Plane; extremely sensitive and a perfect vessel of the Divine Being.

Soul, dark night of. *See* DARK NIGHT OF SOUL.

Soul energy. Waves of energy flowing out of the ECK as the fountainhead of the SUGMAD, which are distributed and differentiated through SOUL.

Soul, Law of. SOUL is the manifested individual BEINGNESS of the ECK SPIRIT; It has FREE WILL, opinions, INTELLIGENCE, IMAGINATION, and IMMORTALITY.

Soul mates. *See* TIME TWINS THEORY OF ECK.

Soul Plane. *See* ATMA LOK.

Soul Travel. Movement of the inner CONSCIOUSNESS, which travels through the lower states until It ascends into the ecstatic state (the AWARENESS of the religious experience of BEING); achieved through a series of spiritual exercises known only to the followers of ECKANKAR.

Soul Travel exercises. *See* SPIRITUAL EXERCISES OF ECK.

Sound Current. *See* AUDIBLE LIFE STREAM.

Sound of ECK. *See* AUDIBLE LIFE STREAM.

space god. KAL NIRANJAN, a god over the world of nothingness— space. *See also* KAL NIRANJAN.

space-time. Qualities of the lower worlds along with matter and energy; the results of considerations which SOUL can make, or agree upon, with Itself or others; limitations of the lower worlds below the SOUL PLANE.

speaking in unknown tongues. A step on the spiritual path; another part of the phenomena of the negative, or KAL, forces.

Spirit. The feeling, or the energy, which the SUGMAD gives off to make the worlds function; the sustaining power of the SUGMAD; the ECK, which is not the SUGMAD, ITSELF, but that which flows out of IT, being in the whole of all things, here and now: true reality.

Spirit, Law of. SPIRIT, in Itself, is the principle of increase; future conditions grow out of present conditions; there is always something more to come, another experience to experience.

spirito-material worlds. The five planes of matter, energy, time, and space which lie below the SOUL PLANE. *See* LOWER PLANES.

Spirit power. The principal factor, the prime action, the all in all in the whole CREATION; the life and SOUL of everything; the electrical force that makes matter move; the ECK.

Spirit rays. SOULS; they reside in HU's continuum of forms throughout all planes and in all times and sustain the whole CREATION, extending from the highest to the lowest sphere.

spiritual cities. The seven cities which are on earth to help this world. *See also* AGAM DES; AKEVIZ; DAMCAR; KIMTAVED; NAMPAK; SAT DHAM; SHAMBALLA.

spiritual consciousness. Truth realized via ECKANKAR; CONSCIOUSNESS of the presence of the SUGMAD, the activity of IT; being aware of and living in closeness with the supreme SPIRIT.

spiritual discipline. To yield the inner self to the one divine ECK.

Spiritual Exercises of ECK. Spiritual exercises known to the followers of ECKANKAR, the Ancient Science of Soul Travel, which promote the movement of the inner CONSCIOUSNESS known as SOUL TRAVEL.

Spiritual Eye. *See* TISRA TIL.

spiritual freedom. Liberation from the WHEEL OF THE EIGHTY-FOUR, or wheel of life, KARMA, REINCARNATION, and from all ills of the mortal life; the ability to come and go among the worlds of the

S

139

COSMIC ORDER as desired; JIVAN MUKTI, SPIRITUAL LIBERATION here and now.

Spiritual Growth, Law of. Truth has to be continually rediscovered, reformed, and transformed; the same truth has to be experienced in ever-new forms.

spiritual hierarchy. Beginning with the SUGMAD, followed by the ECK and the MAHANTA, the LIVING ECK MASTERS, the ADEPTS of the Order of the Vairagi, the Lords of each plane within the higher worlds, and the guardians of the SHARIYAT-KI-SUGMAD. Over the lower worlds SUGMAD placed KAL NIRANJAN, the Lord of the negative worlds; then came the LORDS OF KARMA, the DEVAS (ANGELS), planetary spirits, BHUTS, ELEMENTALS; then came man and all the creatures subordinate to him: fish, animals, reptiles, plants, and stones.

spirituality. That which is caught, not taught; the life impulses received through learning the secrets of spirituality at the feet of an ECK MASTER.

spiritual law. Each SOUL must personally seek to become a clear CHANNEL through which the HOLY SPIRIT can flow to the outer world.

spiritual liberation. The recognition of ENLIGHTENMENT within the state of SOUL Consciousness in the ATMA SARUP, SOUL BODY; the state of Self-Awareness; SELF-REALIZATION; recognition that the universal mission is being a CO-WORKER with the SUGMAD.

spiritual Master. In ECKANKAR, one who has gained the strength and love by passing through the rituals of GOD-REALIZATION and is an ADEPT in the Ancient Order of the Vairagi; although he lives in this world, he is not of it, but conforms to the laws of nature and the social order in which he dwells.

spiritual travelers. The ECK MASTERS, the ADEPTS of the Ancient Order of the Vairagi. *See also* VAIRAGI ADEPTS.

spiritual understanding. That state of SPIRITUAL UNFOLDMENT wherein there is the recognition that the chief goal is to become a vehicle for God, whether in the physical or in the higher PLANES.

spiritual unfoldment. The step-by-step unfolding by SOUL of AWARENESS of Itself and Its relationship with SPIRIT and the SUGMAD.

spiritual wisdom. That stage of unfoldment on the spiritual path of ECKANKAR wherein SOUL has the opportunity to study the scriptures known as the SHARIYAT-KI-SUGMAD and to converse with the nine unknown ECK MASTERS.

spiritual worlds. The PLANES, or worlds, from the Fifth, or SOUL, PLANE up to the SUGMAD: the ALAKH LOK, the ALAYA LOK, the HUKIKAT LOK, the AGAM LOK, the ANAMI LOK, the SUGMAD World, and the SUGMAD, the OCEAN OF LOVE AND MERCY.

sraosha. *srah-OH-shah* The eighth ray, or way, the supreme SUGMAD has of making ITSELF known to man; the ECK, that which can be heard, the AUDIBLE LIFE STREAM. *See also* AMESHA SPENTAS.

Sri. *SREE* A variation of the title *sire,* used for those who have attained the KINGDOM OF GOD.

states of being. *See* ATTITUDES, LAW, OF.

states of consciousness. The four states with which SOUL works in following the spiritual path of ECKANKAR: SPIRIT, SUBCONSCIOUS, MIND, and body.

stratosphere. The layer, or world, which extends for miles into the sky. The ozone layer is the objective side, and the subjective side is the plane, or region, called DASWAN DWAR in ECKANKAR.

subconscious mind. The unconscious, unknown attitudes and habits; the negativeness of the reactive mind; the uncontrolled MIND; that which enslaves SOUL.

subtle body. The SUKHSHAM SHARIR; the NURI SARUP, or LIGHT BODY, the ASTRAL BODY; when the PHYSICAL BODY dies, the subtle body remains as the instrument of expression on the ASTRAL PLANE.

Sudar Singh. *SOO-dahr SING* The LIVING ECK MASTER who lived in Allahabad, India, and taught PEDDAR ZASKQ, also known as PAUL TWITCHELL.

141

SUGMAD. *SOOG-mahd* The formless, all-embracing, impersonal, infinite, the OCEAN OF LOVE AND MERCY; from IT flows all
life, all truth, all reality; all WISDOM, love, and power; all visible
lords of all regions are ITS MANIFESTATIONS; IT takes many forms
in order that ITS purposes may be carried out in all CREATIONS,
but none of them express ITS totality, as IT remains formless,
impersonal, and all-pervading; the universal SPIRIT, universal
life; the supreme God; what there is and all there is, so that no
name can really be given IT except the poetic name of God; IT
is neither old nor new, great nor small, shaped nor shapeless;
having no opposite, IT is what opposites have in common; IT is
the reason why there is no white without black and no form
apart from emptiness; it has an inside called NIRGUNA, which is
to say IT has no qualities and nothing can be said or thought
about IT, and an outside called SAGUNA, which is to say that IT
may be considered as eternal reality, CONSCIOUSNESS, and joy.

SUGMAD trinity. Isness, the creative moment; nowness, the present, the preservation of the moment; hereness, the present
state of life.

Sukhsham Desh. *SOOK-shahm DEHSH* A name for the ASTRAL
WORLD.

Sukhsham mind. *SOOK-shahm* That MIND which works mainly
on the ASTRAL PLANE.

Sukhsham Sarup. Also Sukhsham Sharir. *See* SUBTLE BODY.

Sultan-ul-Ashkar. *SOOL-tahn-ool-AHSH-kahr* Another name
for the ECK. *See also* SHABDA DHUN.

Sumer. *SOO-mehr* One of three peaks seen from the city of MER
KAILASH on the MENTAL PLANE; the other two are KAILASH and MER.

Sumeru. *SOO-mehr-oo* The sacred mountain in the mythlology of
the Ural-Altaic people.

Sun Worlds. Subplanes which lie between the PHYSICAL PLANE and
the true ASTRAL PLANE. *See also* LIGHTNING WORLDS; MOON WORLDS.

Supaku. *soo-pah-KOO* The LIVING ECK MASTER during one of the high periods of the civilization of ATLANTIS; helped to compile a number of the herbs, roots, seeds, flowers, and plants which were researched in the government health laboratories.

Supreme Being. *See* SUGMAD.

Supreme consciousness. That which is omnipresent, omniscient, and omnipotent; the all in all, the SUGMAD.

Supreme Deity. *See* SUGMAD.

supreme doctrine. The VOICE OF THE SUGMAD, the ECK.

supreme infinite essence. The ECK; composed of pure SPIRIT; universal Spirit, moving forth in a living stream, vibrating through all worlds, entering in and vitalizing all that exists; the dynamic life of everything that lives; impersonal, all-permeating, omnipresent, all-sustaining; the life, the very existence of all.

supreme intelligence. SPIRIT, or the ECK, working as the CREATIVE PRINCIPLE through the whole; the harmonious unity of action which works in an all-knowing, forwarding movement for the welfare of all.

supreme principle. *See* SUGMAD.

supreme Spirit. The ECK, the MANIFESTATION of the supreme SUGMAD.

Surat. *soo-RAHT* Another name for SOUL; JIVATMA; ATMA; or Tuza.

Surat Abhyas. *soo-RAHT AHB-hyahz* One of five Spiritual Exercises in ECK for lifting SOUL out of the body to move into the higher worlds. *See also* SPIRITUAL EXERCISES OF ECK.

Surati Lok. *soo-RAH-tee LOHK* The plane of the Mountain world where the ECK CHELAS study in the TEMPLE OF GOLDEN WISDOM under the ECK MASTER FUBBI QUANTZ in the KATSUPARI MONASTERY in northern Tibet.

Surat Shabda. *soo-RAHT SHAHB-dah* One of the many names for the DIVINE SPIRIT, the HEAVENLY MUSIC, the VADAN, the LOGOS, the WORD, the ECK.

Surat Shabda Yoga. *soo-RAHT SHAHB-dah YOH-gah* The yoga of the SOUND CURRENT; the oldest yoga system known in the history of mankind.

Surat technique. *soo-RAHT* One of the SOUL TRAVEL techniques of ECKANKAR wherein one listens for the Sound.

surrender. *See* SELF-SURRENDER.

Sushumna. *See* CROWN CHAKRA.

sushupti. *soo-SHOOP-tee* The dreamless sleep which is the highest from the separate CONSCIOUSNESS.

Suti Sarup. *SOO-tee sah-ROOP* SUBCONSIOUS body of man. *See also* ETHERIC BODY.

swadharma. *swah-DAHR-mah* Law of one's own life; self-imposed duties.

swadhistana chakra. *swahd-ees-TAH-nah CHAH-krah* The INDRI CHAKRA, or Shat-dal-Kanwal. *See also* KUNDALINI.

swami. *SWAH-mee* The all-pervading lord.

Swasa Sohang. *SWAH-sah SOH-hahng* A spiritual exercise; one of the doors through which one might reach THE ABSOLUTE.

S

sylphs. *See* ELEMENTALS.

syzygy. The name for both of the attributes, the ANIMA and ANIMUS.

T

Tamanata Kop. *tah-mah-NAH-tah KOHP* The TEMPLE OF GOLDEN
WISDOM on the sixth plane, the ALAKH LOK.

Tamaqui. *tah-MAH-kee* A minor ECK MASTER in Germany during
the latter part of the nineteenth century.

tamas. *TAH-mahs* One of the three GUNAS, or attributes of nature;
the guna of darkness, destruction, IGNORANCE, DEATH, and inertia;
taught in the yoga of Patanjali.

tanha. *TAHN-hah* Origin of suffering, which is DESIRE or craving
for finite existence, pleasure, and success.

tanmatra. *tahn-MAH-trah* A primary element, like taste.

tantra. *TAHN-trah* The full, unconditional acceptance of life and
the worlds of CREATION, as they are; worship of the primitive
energy called SHAKTI, which creates and destroys; the KALI cult.

Tao. *DOW* The Chinese word for the way to heaven; one who
follows a spiritual master.

tapas. *TAH-pahs* A word for austerity, penance; the intense
application of spiritual exercises.

Tariqat. *tah-ree-KAHT* A stage of spiritual development which is
the code of the higher spiritual morality and conduct; a practice
which leads to spiritual realization.

tassawar. *TAH-sah-wahr* One of the creative techniques for SOUL TRAVEL where the attention is on the INNER MASTER, his Radiant form or image, and the LIGHT and the Sound.

Tat. *TAHT* The supreme Deity worshiped by the ATLANTEANS.

Tat Tsoks. *TAHT TSOHKS* The cruel king-priests who ruled ATLANTIS with an iron hand.

tattwas. *TAH-twahz* The five elements or ESSENCES of matter. *See also* PRIMARY STATES OF MATTER.

Tejahua. *teh-jah-HOO-ah* An ECK MASTER on the MENTAL PLANE.

tejas. *TEH-jahs* Luster, beauty, and power.

tek. *TEHK* Blind FAITH.

temple of God. Every SOUL manifesting in a body in the lower worlds has the SPIRIT dwelling within, is the Spirit, is a temple of God.

Temples of Golden Wisdom. The spiritual temples which exist on the various PLANES—from the PHYSICAL to the ANAMI LOK; CHELAS of ECKANKAR are taken to the temples in the SOUL BODY to be educated in the DIVINE KNOWLEDGE; the different sections of the SHARIYAT-KI-SUGMAD, the sacred teachings of ECK, are kept at these temples; there are fourteen main temples, one per plane, but also many branch temples on each level.

Tenth Door. The Maha Sunna which lies beyond the nine doors of the lower CREATION up to BRAHM; the SPIRITUAL EYE; the single eye, behind the eyes at a point between the eyebrows. *See also* MAHA SUNNA; TISRA TIL.

Thigala. *thee-GAH-lah* The first twelve-year cycle of the DUODE-NARY CYCLE called the Years of the Fierce Winds. *See also* CYCLES OF TWELVE.

Third Eye. *See* TISRA TIL.

thirty-two facets of ECKANKAR. *See* ECKANKAR, THIRTY-TWO FACETS OF.

Thor's hammer. The swastika, a form of the balanced cross, which is supposed to bring about PURIFICATION, adjustment, and balance by the hard knocks of karma (blows from its whirling ends).

thought. Pure mental action, which is the only possible source from which existing CREATION could ever have come into MANIFESTATION at all; formed only when SPIRIT activates MIND.

three characteristics of the human state of being. Inertia, or movement caused only by inner force; DISINTEGRATION, or conflict between matter and the ECK, which manifests as life; and transformation, or the breaking down of matter into its elements which is then revitalized and used again in another form.

Time Track. The past, present, and future track upon which each individual life is lived while in the LOWER PLANES.

time twins theory of ECK. When SOUL discovers Itself as the ECK, and by becoming the ECK, It has attained the symbol of Its Soul mate; the blending of the masculine and feminine forces within man into one, the oneness with Itself.

Tindor Saki. *TIN-dohr SAH-kee* A renowned ECK MASTER on the fifth, or SOUL, PLANE, who was instrumental in bringing ECK out into the open. As guardian of the SHARIYAT-KI-SUGMAD at the Temple of PARAM AKSHAR his title is the JAGAT GIRI.

Tirich Mir. *TEER-eech MEER* An imposing mountain peak in the HINDU KUSH mountains, near where the ECK MASTER REBAZAR TARZS has his abode.

T

Tirkya Pad. *TEERK-yah PAHD* Variant phrase for TURIYA PAD. *See also* ASTRAL PLANE.

Tirmer, oracle of. *teer-MEER* A craggy, unexplored site sometimes called the Valley of Tirmer, in the VALLEY OF SHANGTA in Tibet where the VOICE OF AKIVASHA is located; the passing of the ROD OF ECK POWER from the LIVING ECK MASTER to his successor occurs here at midnight on October 22.

Tisra Til. *TIZ-rah TIL* The seat of Soul in the waking state, located at a focus between the two eyes, known variously as the Third Eye, the Tenth Door, or as the Spiritual Eye; the window between the physical and spiritual worlds; the pineal gland is the physical equivalent.

Tissot Leins. *tees-SOHT leh-EENS* The Living ECK Master during the sixteenth century in France when the Protestants were being persecuted; responsible for the migration of the Huguenots and other faiths to America.

Tiwaja. *tee-WAH-jah* Also Tiwaga. The gaze of the Master which has the power to uplift and heal all things; one of the mighty acts of God granted to one who becomes a channel for the spiritual power.

Tomo Geshig. *TOH-moh GEH-shig* The ECK Master on the sixth plane, the Alakh Lok, who appears in the form of a halo of light; he studied under Gopal Das in Egypt five thousand years ago, and was the teacher of Lai Tsi, the ECK Master on the Etheric Plane; as guardian of the Shariyat-Ki-Sugmad at the Tamanata Kop Temple of Golden Wisdom, his title is the Sokagampo.

total awareness. The movement of the inner consciousness, Soul, beyond time and space, where all is omniscient, omnipresent, and omnipotent.

Towart Managi. *TOH-wahrt mah-NAH-gee* The ECK Master in charge of the Shariyat-Ki-Sugmad in the Temple of Golden Wisdom on the Mental Plane in the city of Mer Kailash; as guardian his title is the Koji Chanda; an African holy man in ancient days in the country known as Abyssinia.

Translate. Another term for death; to move out of the physical body to another state.

Tretya Yuga. *TREHT-yah YOO-gah* The second, or Silver, Age of the four yugas of a great cycle of time; it lasts for 1,296,000 years and is that period when everything starts to go amiss and every pleasure has some anxiety attached. *See also* Manvantara.

Tribeni. *tree-BEHN-nee* A place where three broad streams meet at the top of the CAUSAL PLANE; the KUMBA MEHLA, a religious fair held every twelve years in India is a reflection of this place.

Trikuti. *tree-KOO-tee* The BRAHM LOK; the MENTAL PLANE; home of the Universal Mind.

Triloki. *tree-LOH-kee* The four regions between the negative pole of CREATION and the ATMA LOK.

trinity of ECK. WISDOM, power, and freedom (various aspects of the SOUND CURRENT).

trinity of ECKANKAR. The SAT GURU, the MAHANTA, the LIVING ECK MASTER; the ECK SATSANG, or his company of followers; and the ECK, or the true name, which is the BANI, or the SOUND CURRENT.

trinity of Kal Niranjan. The Hindu trinity: BRAHMA, VISHNU, and SHIVA; the Western trinity: Father, Son, and Holy Ghost. *See also* TRINITY OF THE HINDUS.

trinity of liberation. The LIVING ECK MASTER, the INITIATION, and the SOUND CURRENT.

trinity of the Deity. LIGHT, Sound, and form; the threefold aspect of God, or the Deity.

trinity of the Hindus. The three CURRENTS flowing out of the BRAHM LOK world: CREATION, or BRAHMA; continuity, or VISHNU; and destruction, or SHIVA; the sons of KAL NIRANJAN or BRAHM, the negative power, and SHAKTI, the female counterpart of the negative; the three subordinate currents flow out of these two great currents into the lower worlds, and to them is attributed the creation of all lower worlds.

trinity of the individual. Each person is spirit, MIND, and body: the three in one, and one in three.

trinity of the SUGMAD. *SOOG-mahd* The three bodies of the MAHANTA: the absolute primordial, the eternal Mahanta, called the clear voice of God, which dwells in the heart of the OCEAN OF

LOVE AND MERCY; the body of glory, the ECK, the COSMIC SPIRIT, the SOUND CURRENT—that which is all life, giving existence to all things; the body of MANIFESTATION, the transformation, the historical Mahanta, the LIVING ECK MASTER in every age, who is the Eternal One, the bodily manifestation of the SUGMAD.

Troglodytes. *TROG-leh-diet* A primitive red race of the Southern continent known as ATLANTIS who were able to survive the destruction; among their descendents today are the Polynesians and American Indians.

tropopause. In ECKANKAR, the BRAHM LOK, or MENTAL PLANE, the fourth region.

troposphere. The ASTRAL WORLD, or SUKHSHAM DESH, the first plane above the PHYSICAL PLANE, or the lowest plane of the FAR COUNTRY. *See also* ASTRAL PLANE.

truth. The ESSENCE, SPIRIT, SOUL, and life of everything that exists or appears to exist, itself unchangeable and immortal; the essence of essences, Spirit of spirits, Soul of Souls, omniscient, omnipotent, formless, boundless, unapproachable, unchangeable; the source and beginning of life, an unlimited ocean of love and WISDOM; the ECK.

Tsong Sikhsa. *TSOHNG SEEK-sah* The title of the guardian of the holy book of ECKANKAR, the SHARIYAT-KI-SUGMAD, at the ANAKAMUDI TEMPLE OF GOLDEN WISDOM on the seventh plane, the ALAYA LOK. MESI GOKARITZ is currently the guardian.

Tulsi Das. *TUHL-see DAHS* One of the pioneers of the FAR COUNTRY, who was a seventeenth-century Hindu mystic poet and follower of ECK.

Tura Yung. *TOO-rah YOONG* The ECK MASTER who is the spiritual head of the TEMPLE OF GOLDEN WISDOM on the SOUL PLANE, the fifth plane.

Turiya Pad. *TOOR-ee-yah PAHD* Also variant form, Tirkya Pad. Another name for the ASTRAL PLANE.

Tuza. *See* SOUL.

Tuzashottama. *TOO-zah-SHOH-tah-mah* *Tuza* means "Soul," *shottama* means "energy"; the Light and the Sound are the basic elements in this Soul energy, which is vibratory. *See also* Shottama.

twelve-year cycle. *See* cycles of twelve.

Twitchell, Paul. The Mahanta, the Living ECK Master from 1965 until 1971 when he translated from the physical; he brought the modern teachings of ECKANKAR to the peoples of the world through his many books, lectures, and writings; as the spiritual head of ECKANKAR, he brought new life and hope to thousands. *See also* Paulji; Peddar Zaskq.

two faces of the Master. The Inner Master, who is always with his chelas, and the Outer Master of ECKANKAR, who writes, lectures, and teaches the outer studies to his followers.

T

U

udghata. *ood-GAH-tah* The act of opening the curtain of the higher worlds.

udgita. *ood-GEE-tah* One of the sound methods of the MENTAL PLANE; the chanting of AUM.

Uighur Empire. *WEE-guhr* The empire of the fifth ROOT RACE, the ARYANS, in central Asia in the Gobi Desert; a highly developed civilization which was the center of the world in its day and had as its capital city KHARA KHOTA. It had previously been a province of LEMURIA.

Ulemans. *OO-leh-mahnz* A race which presently occupies the planet of Jupiter and will descend upon the earth and other planets throughout the solar system to occupy them with absolute ruling power; the next race which will follow the present, or Aryan, race. *See also* ROOT RACES.

Ultimate Being. *See* SUGMAD.

ultimate experience. *See* GOD-REALIZATION.

ultimate reality. The absolute SOUL we strive for in the highest region of God, that nameless world wherein dwells that wondrous Deity whose body is the universal Soul of all things; the WORD of God, or truth; the SUGMAD.

unconscious. The no-mind, no-thought area; freedom from ATTACHMENT to thought; the top of the MENTAL PLANE, the ETHERIC PLANE;

153

the source of primitive thought, a very thin line between the MENTAL body and the SOUL body.

undines. *See* ELEMENTALS.

union with God. In ECK, the CHELA becomes the CO-WORKER with God and not one with IT; SOUL becomes one with the ESSENCE, not the GODHEAD ITSELF; becoming the Co-worker with God is the way to reach GOD-REALIZATION.

Unity, Law of. The seventh law of the physical universe; thinking in the whole instead of the parts. *See also* LAWS OF THE PHYSICAL UNIVERSE.

unity of ECK. All the FUNCTIONS OF LIFE come out of the ECK, which is the unity in the midst of diversity and multiplicity, and preexist in the SUGMAD.

universal Law of Compensation. *See* KARMA, LAW OF.

universal Law of God. Each half of a cycle of the wave from the ECK eternally gives to the other half for regiving; God forever unfolds into many for the purpose of refolding into the one.

Universal Mind. *See* OMKAR; TRIKUTI.

universal principle. No effect can be produced except by the operation of an adequate cause.

universal Sound Current. *See* DIVINE SPIRIT; ECK.

universal Spirit. *See* DIVINE SPIRIT.

universal Spirit of HU. The primary, positive factor, the feeling and thought of the pure Spirit of life; the first positive factor in the whole CREATION, or SPIRIT; the invisible power which concentrates the primordial ether into forms and endows them with various modes of motion; the Sound.

Unmani Dhun. *oon-MAH-nee DOON* The TENTH DOOR, or THIRD EYE; the sound which is heard in this place; one of the SPIRITUAL EXERCISES OF ECK. *See also* TISRA TIL.

uparti. *oo-PAHR-tee* The freedom from ceremonial worship; indifference to sensual pleasures.

upasana. *oo-pah-SAH-nah* Devotion or worship; also includes prayer.

upaya. *oo-PAH-yah* A device for the spiritual seeker to use to move into the higher states; like a raft or boat to get across a river.

Uri. *OO-ree* The city on the ETHERIC PLANE, or BHANWAR GUPHA, where many essential parts of the spiritual ESSENCE for the worlds below are put together, and the seeds, or SOULS (unmanifested atoms), are prepared to be sent into the lower worlds for experiences.

Uturat. *OO-too-raht* The second month of the ECK-VIDYA calendar, February, the days of love, the MONTH OF THE BLOODSTONE. This JOURNEY OF SOUL brings great concern for love, companionship, and wealth.

U

V

Vadan. *VAH-dahn* The primal music of the universe; the music of ECK, heard internally; the WORD of IT, the SUGMAD; the ESSENCE of life.

Vahana. *vah-HAH-nah* Vehicle; carrier of ECK or the MESSAGE OF ECK; the ECK missionary. *See also* VAHANA MARG.

Vahana Marg. *vah-HAH-nah MAHRG* The order of the missionary; the INITIATE gives of himself to the ECK as a carrier of the MESSAGE OF ECK into the world and among the masses of mankind. These are the preachers and true messengers of the spiritual truths of ECKANKAR.

vairag. *vie-RAHG* Nonattachment; renouncing of material things; having mental DETACHMENT from worldly DESIRES and things; SOUL lives forever by giving, not by receiving; the opposite of MOHA, or ATTACHMENT.

Vairagi Adepts. *vie-RAH-gee AD-ehpts* The ancient and long-lived ADEPTS of ECK; the mystic Adepts of the HIMALAYAS, the Adepts of the Vairagi; along with yet higher entities they form an ESOTERIC group whose existence has been known to the mystics and occultists in every age; the "just men" of the sacred scriptures in the West, made perfect.

Vaita Danu. *vie-EE-tah DAH-noo* The LIVING ECK MASTER who lived during the time of Alexander the Great. He lived for more than 150 years. His successor was JU CHIAO.

Vajra Manjushri. *VAHJ-rah mahn-JOO-shree* The ECK MASTER about 700 B.C. in Persia who was executed by King Hakhamanish I through the instigation of a priest of Mithra; he now teaches in the CAUSAL WORLD.

Valley of Shangta. *shahng-TAH* The valley near the KATSUPARI MONASTERY in northern Tibet where the ECK MASTERS gather at the passing of the ROD OF ECK POWER from a departing Master to his successor. *See also* TIRMER, ORACLE OF; VOICE OF AKIVASHA.

vanity. Self-admiration; the abnormal exaggeration of the faculty of interest in self or the faculty of MIND which gives the power of AWARENESS of SOUL; also self-righteousness; destroys all sense of humor; in ECK also called AHANKARA; bigotry, self-assertion, obtrusive show of wealth or power, bossiness, scolding, fault-finding, liking publicity, making a show of religion, and being noisy about giving to CHARITY; the opposite of HUMILITY. *See also* DINTA; FIVE PASSIONS OF THE MIND.

Vardrup. *VAHR-droop* The LIVING ECK MASTER who came from Germany to the Americas to give spiritual aid, not only to the Indian chiefs during the early conquest of Mexico and the southwestern United States, but to many Europeans and Asiatics as well.

Varkas. *VAHR-kahz* The fierce kings who were the rulers of the HYPERBOREANS, the second ROOT RACE; their awful powers were used to conquer their foes and their subjects, while some of them conquered time and lived for centuries. *See also* ZUAJIRS.

Varnatmik. *vahr-NAHT-meek* That part of the spiritual teachings which can be written and spoken; the Sound which breaks into many sounds in the lower worlds. *See also* DHUNATMIK.

Varuna. *vah-ROO-nah* The MAHANTA, the LIVING ECK MASTER as he appeared to the ancient ARYANS; one of the oldest Hindu gods.

vayu. *VAH-yoo* Air and related subjects; one of the TATTWAS, the five PRIMARY STATES OF MATTER, the others being AGNI, PRITHVI, JAL, and AKASH.

Vedas. *VEH-dahz* Collection of ancient Hindu hymns; sacred scriptures.

vehicle. That Soul who has unfolded to the AWARENESS of Itself and can be used by the ECK as the means of expressing Itself in the lower worlds; such as the LIVING ECK MASTER and the CHELAS of ECK.

Venus. The planet in whose capital city, RETZ, there is an ECK TEMPLE OF GOLDEN WISDOM.

vibhuta. *vee-BOO-tah* The ability to manifest great psychic powers.

vibrations. Wavelengths in the specialized stream of SPIRIT; the whole life of any individual is one great wavelength; music and electricity are also wavelengths, as is every particle in the lower worlds; the wavelengths of the ECK. *See* VIBRATIONS, LAW OF.

Vibrations, Law of. The fourth law of the universe which governs all the influences such as wavelengths, outflows, inflows, CAUSE AND EFFECT, and the harmonics of the movement of sound. *See also* KARMA, LAW OF; LAWS OF THE PHYSICAL UNIVERSE.

vibratory actinics. The action of LIGHT AND SOUND rays; the energy which SOUL uses to travel in the other worlds.

vidya. *VEE-dyah* Knowledge. *See also* ATMA VIDYA; AVIDYA; ECK-VIDYA; GUPTA-VIDYA; PARA VIDYA; PRADA VIDYA.

Vi-Guru. *VIE-goo-roo* The MAHANTA, the highest of all SPIRITUAL MASTERS; supreme GURU, or spiritual teacher.

vigyan. *VEEG-yahn* ESOTERIC knowledge.

Vigyan Dhan. *VEEG-yahn DAHN* One of the SPIRITUAL EXERCISES OF ECK; contemplating in silence the Radiant form of the Master.

vihara. *vee-HAH-rah* Dwelling place of CONSCIOUSNESS.

vijnana. *veej-NAH-nah* CONSCIOUSNESS; to apprehend, or bring into mental MANIFESTATION, an inner experience.

vipula. *VEE-poo-lah* An ECK sage.

virtues, five. *See* FIVE VIRTUES.

Vishnu. *VEESH-noo* Second member of the Hindu trinity; the existence of a cycle of action or continuity. *See also* TRINITY OF THE HINDUS.

vishudha chakra. *vees-HOO-dah CHAH-krah* The sixteen-petaled lotus at the throat; the seat of the ether element; the COLOR is purple. *See also* KANTH CHAKRA.

visualization. Seeing in the IMAGINATION; a kind of feeling, believing, and accepting. *See also* INNER VISION.

Viswapati. *vee-swah-PAH-tee* Title meaning lord of the world; great ECK MASTER. Paul's fictional variation of the MAHANTA, used only in *The Way of Dharma.*

viveka. *vee-VEH-kah* The first step in ECKANKAR; right DISCRIMINATION; being able to discriminate between what will be good for spiritual advancement or would be wasting time; the opposite of LOBHA, GREED. *See also* BAIBEK; FIVE PASSIONS OF THE MIND.

vohu-mano. *VOH-hoo-MAH-noh* One of the six rays of light from the Divine; the good MIND, DIVINE WISDOM, pure mindedness. *See also* AMESHA SPENTAS.

Voice of Akivasha. *ah-kee-VAH-shah* The oracle, until the first of this century, at a craggy, unexplored site called the Oracle of Tirmer in the VALLEY OF SHANGTA in northern Tibet. It is here that the ROD OF ECK POWER is passed from the departing LIVING ECK MASTER to his successor on October 22, at midnight; sometimes called the Voice, or Oracle, of Tirmer. *See also* TIRMER, ORACLE OF.

voice of everlasting law. The LAW OF CAUSE AND EFFECT put into action at the beginning of the universe. *See also* KARMA, LAW OF.

Voice of HU. The SPIRIT; often known as the SUGMAD, the true name of God in the upper realms. *See also* LAW OF HU, PRINCIPLE OF HU; UNIVERSAL SPIRIT OF HU.

voice of silence. The Sound which is the ECK; the small still voice; the primal chord; the PRIMAL WORD; the Voice of the supreme CREATOR.

Voice of the SUGMAD. *SOOG-mahd* The DHUNATMIK, the Sound which cannot be spoken; It has no written symbol; the music of the SUGMAD.

Voice of Tirmer. *See* VOICE OF AKIVASHA.

Void, the. The OCEAN OF LOVE AND MERCY; the original place of all things; emptiness in its own nature; being devoid of self-distinctiveness and independent from the elements which compose it; a blank; everything else is relative to it, but it is not in relation to other things. Not to be confused with the void of the Buddhists which is below the SOUL PLANE. There are lesser voids, or dark, empty areas, between each of the LOWER PLANES.

Volapuk. *voh-lah-POOK* A Silent One, capable of expression without limits.

vyapakkatva. *vyah-pahk-KAHT-vah* OMNIPRESENCE.

W

Wah Z. *WAH ZEE* The spiritual name of SRI HAROLD KLEMP, the LIVING ECK MASTER who was given the ROD OF ECK POWER of the MAHANTA at midnight on October 22, 1981, in the VALLEY OF SHANGTA at the ORACLE OF TIRMER. *See also* KLEMP, HAROLD.

waking dream. A form of the GOLDEN-TONGUED WISDOM, which is a form of the ECK-VIDYA working in your daily life; occurs while we are awake among the seemingly meaningless and insignificant events of our daily life. It is having the degree of consciousness expanding outwardly in concentric circles around you, reaching further and further to encompass the knowledge you need to make better decisions to run your life.

wallis. *WAHL-eez* Prophet or a holy man.

Way of the Eternal. The SHARIYAT-KI-SUGMAD, the sacred books of ECKANKAR, which are placed in the TEMPLES OF GOLDEN WISDOM on the various PLANES under the protection of the ECK MASTERS, and which contain the sacred and secret truths taught the ECK CHELAS in their SOUL BODIES.

Wayshower. *See* MAHANTA.

Wei Wu Wei. *WAY woo WAY* In Chinese mysticism, this means to do without doing, to act without action; let God be God in you.

Wheel of Awagawan. *ah-WAH-gah-wahn* The coming and going; the agelong cycle of births and DEATHS, transmigration, and the REINCARNATION OF SOUL. *See also* WHEEL OF THE EIGHTY-FOUR.

Wheel of Samsara. *See* WHEEL OF THE EIGHTY-FOUR.

Wheel of the Eighty-Four. The twelve paths SOUL must experience in Its coming and going in the lower worlds; the twelve paths, or divisions, of the wheel of becoming; Soul spends eighty-four LACS in each birth sign, and each lac is equivalent to one hundred thousand years; eighty-four lacs amount to eight million four hundred thousand years. *See also* JOURNEY OF SOUL; WHEEL OF AWAGAWAN.

will of the SUGMAD. *SOOG-mahd* That will which is the will of the whole; man can become in HARMONY with this will by bringing about peace and harmony within himself through the decision by his own will to do so; then, even though he seems to be limited, his will becomes absorbed into the whole, and so his will becomes the will of the SUGMAD. *See also* DIVINE WILL.

willpower. The divine willpower is the whole; the human willpower is the part; in the whole, it is the almighty, or ECK, POWER, and in the individual it is a limited power; the truth is the will of God.

wisdom. The intuitive wisdom which dawns when the MIND is stilled and SOUL makes contact with the COSMIC LIGHT AND SOUND; knowledge gained directly from looking and knowing in the SPIRITUAL WORLDS.

wisdom of ECK. The secret wisdom which is collected, collated, and set down in a permanent form in the SHARIYAT-KI-SUGMAD, a holy book divided into approximately twelve books; each section is placed in a TEMPLE OF GOLDEN WISDOM in the many planes throughout the universes of God.

wisdom of God. Made up of the prime forces of personal FAITH, enthusiasm, and love of SOUL.

wisdom plane. The STRATOSPHERE, or MENTAL PLANE, as it is known to the Vedantists.

Wisdom Ray. The first of the ten forces, or rays, of the ECK which are sent out to the worlds below by the SUGMAD through the ECK.

Word, the. The eternal Voice; the true BANI; SHABDA; the LIGHT; the real life and true light, the true nectar which is the ECK; that which is within; the name, the ECK, MUSIC OF THE SPHERES, the QUALIMA, NADA, ABSOLUTE TRUTH, the divine melody.

worlds of the chela. The three worlds are: the HUMAN CONSCIOUSNESS, the psychic CONSCIOUSNESS, and the SPIRITUAL CONSCIOUSNESS; all three are lived in simultaneously and singularly.

Wu Tenna. *WOO TEHN-nah* An ECK MASTER who is the spiritual head of the TEMPLE OF GOLDEN WISDOM on the MENTAL PLANE.

Y

yagya. *YAHG-yah* Sacrifice.

Yahveh. *YAH-veh* One of the Hebrew names assigned to the god who was first a tribal deity of the Jews, but later proclaimed lord over all gods and worlds; the supreme law giver, the commander of all the armies of Israel. *See also* ADONAI.

Yama. *YAH-mah* The KING OF THE DEAD; the judge who judges every individual according to his deeds; all uninitiated SOULS must pass through his court. Also, in yoga, one part of the eightfold path. *See also* DHARAM RAYA.

Yama Dutas. *YAH-mah DOO-tahz* The messengers of DEATH, the ANGELS OF DEATH, or the dark ANGELS; the messengers of YAMA, the King of the Dead. *See also* DHARAM RAYA.

Yaubl Sacabi. *YEEOW-buhl sah-KAH-bee* The ECK MASTER among the Mycenaeans (who invaded Greece during the period between 2000–1700 B.C.); he was the leading figure among the Greek mystery cults and is now the guardian of the SHARIYAT-KI-SUGMAD, the sacred book of ECK, in the spiritual city of AGAM DES, the home of the ESHWAR-KHANEWALE, the God-eaters.

Yavata. *yah-VAH-tah* The Yavata is an ECK MASTER teaching on the inner planes. The odor of sweet musk, the sound of violins, and a white light indicate his presence.

Yigerta. *yee-GEHR-tah* The fourth twelve-year cycle of the DOUDE-NARY CYCLE called the Years of the Beautiful Flowers. *See also* CYCLES OF TWELVE.

167

yin/yang. *yin/yahng* Yin is the feminine, the negative principle; yang is the male, the positive principle.

Yreka. *yuh-REE-kah* The tunnel between the ETHERIC PLANE and SOUL PLANE; the dark area through which SOUL must travel to reach the Soul Plane and SELF-REALIZATION.

yuga. *YOO-gah* A great CYCLE OF TIME. *See also* KALPA; MANVANTARA; MAHAYUGA.

Yuont-Na. *yeeownt-NAY* An ECK MASTER who lived and taught in the city of KHARA KHOTA; he now is a teacher of the SHARIYAT-KI-SUGMAD on the ASTRAL PLANE.

Yu Rantga. *yoo RAHNT-gah* A Chinese ECK MASTER; the LIVING ECK MASTER in the middle and latter part of the nineteenth century in the Gobi desert who brought the Chinese back many of their old religious customs; now he works on the ASTRAL PLANE.

Y

Z

Z. *ZEE* Spiritual name for Sri Harold Klemp. *See also* Wah Z.

Zadok. *ZAH-dohk* The Living ECK Master in the country of Judea, north of Jerusalem, who founded a mystical organization which exists today in the Middle East and accepts the Mahanta; he taught a man named Jesus the basic fundamentals of ECK; out of this knowledge of ECK came what we know today as Christianity.

Zarathustra. *See* Zoroaster.

Zaskq, Peddar. *See* Twitchell, Paul; Peddar Zaskq.

Zezirath. *ZEHZ-eer-ahth* The old city of Zezirath is near the ruins of Memphis in Egypt.

zikar. *ZIE-kahr* Chanting, or repetition, of the holy word.

ziquin. *ZEE-kwin* In the Amdo language, *zi* means "above," *quin* means "five;" above the five planes; the reading of the ECK-Vidya from the Fifth, or Soul, Plane.

Zoas. *ZOH-ahz* The four Zoas (laws) of ECKANKAR for the Mahdis, the initiate of the Fifth Circle, are (1) The Mahdis shall not use alcohol, tobacco, drugs, gamble, or be gluttonous in any way. No Mahdis shall be existent on the animal level. He is a leader, and he must fix his attention above the psychology of the brute. (2) The Mahdis shall not speak with tongue of vanity or deceit or unhappiness, criticize the actions of others, blame others for wrongdoings, quarrel, fight, or inflict injury. He shall

169

at all times be respectful and courteous to his fellowman and show great COMPASSION and happiness. (3) The Mahdis shall have HUMILITY, love, and freedom from all bonds of creeds. He shall be free from the laws of karma which snare him with boastfulness and vanity. He shall have love for all people and all creatures of the SUGMAD. (4) The Mahdis must preach the MESSAGE OF ECK at all times, and prove to the world that he is an example of purity and happiness. He must show that the disciple in the human body must have a Master in the human body.

zodiac. *ZOH-dee-ak* The twelve signs of ASTROLOGY which influence the PHYSICAL BODY and character traits of man. *See also* JOURNEY OF SOUL; WHEEL OF THE EIGHTY-FOUR.

Zohar people. *ZOH-hahr* The seventh ROOT RACE who will come from a far distant planet to colonize the world after the destruction in the twenty-first and twenty-second centuries, but they will fail and after several centuries will withdraw.

Zoroaster. *ZOH-roh-as-tehr* The Persian AVATAR who taught SOUL TRAVEL a few hundred years before the coming of Christ and his followers.

Zrephs. *ZREHFS* The flowering gardens of the ASTRAL WORLD near the ASTRAL MUSEUM and the TEMPLE OF GOLDEN WISDOM there.

Zuajirs. *zoo-AH-jeerz* The Hyperborean priests who were more cruel than their masters, the fierce VARKAS kings, in ruling the second ROOT RACE at the time when man was hardly out of the jungle. *See also* KAI-KUAS.

Z

How to Learn More about ECKANKAR

People want to know the secrets of life and death. In response to this need Sri Harold Klemp, today's spiritual leader of ECKANKAR, and Paul Twitchell, its modern-day founder, have written special monthly discourses which reveal the Spiritual Exercises of ECK—to lead Soul in a direct way to God.

Those who wish to study ECKANKAR can receive these special monthly discourses which give clear, simple instructions for the spiritual exercises. The first annual series of discourses is *The ECK Dream 1 Discourses*. Mailed each month, the discourses will offer insight into your dreams and what they mean to you.

The techniques in these discourses, when practiced twenty minutes a day, are likely to prove survival beyond death. Many have used them as a direct route to Self-Realization, where one learns his mission in life. The next stage, God Consciousness, is the joyful state wherein Soul becomes the spiritual traveler, an agent for God. The underlying principle one learns is this: Soul exists because God loves It.

Membership in ECKANKAR includes:

1. Twelve monthly lessons of *The ECK Dream 1 Discourses*, with such titles as: "Dreams—The Bridge to Heaven," "The Dream Master," "How to Interpret Your Dreams," and "Dream Travel to Soul Travel." You may study them alone at home or in a class with others.
2. The *Mystic World*, a quarterly newsletter with a Wisdom Note and articles by the Living ECK Master. In it are also letters and articles from students of ECKANKAR around the world.
3. Special mailings to keep you informed of upcoming ECKANKAR seminars and activities worldwide, new study materials available from ECKANKAR, and more.
4. The opportunity to attend ECK Satsang classes and book discussions with others in your community.
5. Initiation eligibility.
6. Attendance at certain chela meetings at ECK seminars.

How to Find out More

To request membership in ECKANKAR using your credit card (or for a free booklet on membership) call (612) 544-0066 between 8 a.m. and 5 p.m., central time.

There May Be an
ECKANKAR Study Group near You

ECKANKAR offers a variety of local and international activities for the spiritual seeker. With hundreds of study groups worldwide, ECKANKAR is near you! Many areas have ECKANKAR Centers where you can browse through the books in a quiet, unpressured environment, talk with others who share an interest in this ancient teaching, and attend beginning discussion classes on how to gain the attributes of Soul: wisdom, power, love, and freedom.

Around the world, ECKANKAR study groups offer special one-day or weekend seminars on the basic teachings of ECKANKAR. Check your phone book under **ECKANKAR**, or call **(612) 544-0066** for membership information and the location of the ECKANKAR Center or study group nearest you. Or write **ECKANKAR, Att: Information, P.O. Box 27300, Minneapolis, MN 55427 U.S.A.**

☐ Please send me information on the nearest ECKANKAR discussion or study group in my area.

☐ Please send me more information about membership in ECKANKAR, which includes a twelve-month spiritual study of dreams.

Please type or print clearly   941

Name_____

Street_____ Apt. #_____

City_____ State/Prov._____

Zip/Postal Code_____Country_____

(Our policy: Your name and address are held in strict confidence. We do not rent or sell our mailing lists. Nor will anyone call on you. Our purpose is only to show people the ECK way home to God.)